COPING WITH SPECIAL NEEDS: A GUIDE FOR NEW TEACHERS

CROOM HELM SERIES ON SPECIAL EDUCATION NEEDS: POLICY, PRACTICES AND SOCIAL ISSUES

General Editor: Len Barton, Westhill College, Birmingham

SPECIAL EDUCATION AND SOCIAL INTERESTS
Edited by Len Barton and Sally Tomlinson

CONTENTS

For Lois, Isaac, Jessica and Rachel
and the many pupils, students and colleagues
who have helped me since I started to teach.

Chapter One

PREPARING TO TEACH CHILDREN WITH SPECIAL NEEDS

Soon after I was appointed as Lecturer in Special and Remedial Education, two students came and asked me to give some lectures on the secondary P.G.C.E. course. We were then running an extensive in-service and higher degree programme for experienced teachers and a year long optional course for B.Ed Primary Students. But in common with many other Teacher Training Institutions (Clunies-Ross and Wimhurst:1983), there was no provision for Secondary Teachers on initial training.

A meeting was called to see what kind of strategy we should adopt. The students did not want a recipe book approach. A few practical hints might be useful, but they had already had enough lectures on making worksheets.

They wanted to know something of the intellectual debate within the Special Education field, so they could form their own ideas and their own practical approaches. They wanted to know what really happened and they wanted illustrative case histories.

Over 50 P.G.C.E.'s attended that first meeting. Many knew disabled adults and children and felt they would like to be involved in their education. Others had helped out in the Remedial Departments of their own schools when they were in the Sixth Form. For a few, the satisfaction of enabling a twelve year old to read had been a decisive factor in choosing teaching as a career. Yet for all the interest our discussion provoked, there was an air of unreality for at least one of the students. She asked. "But surely _we_ won't have to teach these children, will we ?"

According to the most recent Committee of Enquiry into the Education of Handicapped Children and Young People, the Warnock Report (H.M.S.O.:1978), as many as 20 per cent of the child population could be deemed to have "Special Educational Needs" at some time in their schooling. Some people tend to think of special needs as if it was mainly concerned with teaching the blind and deaf. In fact, fewer than one child in 400 has visual or hearing impairment. Many more of the children in special schools have "severe" learning difficulties ("the mentally handicapped") or "moderate" learning difficulties. But only one child in 50 has gone to a Special School. According to Warnock most of the children with "special needs" go to ordinary Primary and Secondary Schools. Most of these are referred to by Warnock as having "mild learning difficulties".

In the past these children were known by a plethora of labels - "Slow Learners", "Backward Readers" or "Remedial Children". The teachers responsible for them were known as the "Remedial Department", the "Opportunities or Progress Departments" or the "Remove". And there were a number of different ways of organising them. They could be picked out according to teacher recommendation or objective IQ and reading test scores. They could be put in a Slow Learners' class for "academic" lessons but join the rest of the year for practical subjects and P.E. Or they could be based in a mixed ability class and "withdrawn" for extra English, extra Maths or both. Remedial provision might last for the first two years or it might extend throughout the age range.

The Warnock Committee attempted to cut through this confusion. They drew an analogy between children in ordinary schools who had learning difficulties and those in special schools. Both groups, in their view, required special education. They promoted the use of the term "Special Educational Needs" and they included the 2 per cent of the population presently in Special Schools and the 20 per cent of those in ordinary schools in this. Previous labels and organisational approaches were to be superseded:

> At present "remedial" groups include children with a variety of difficulties which, though different in origin are frequently treated alike ..There are children who have been absent from school and need to make up work which they have missed; children with physical or sensory disabilities, sometimes temporary,

> sometimes permanent; children with varying degrees of learning difficulties and children who need to be withdrawn from the normal class for specific purposes. The term "remedial", like the term "treatment", suggests that these children have something wrong with them that can be put right. It is true that some of them are suffering only a temporary learning difficulty.. Others, however, require special help and support throughout their school lives .. We conclude that a meaningful distinction between remedial and special education can no longer be maintained.

Although the change in terminology from Remedial to Special Education has been widely accepted there are still doubts and criticisms.

It has been argued that insofar as all children are individuals, no child's needs can be any more "special" than any other's. A distinction based on IQ score or reading age would create an artificial division within what is clearly a continuum. The actual scores used by the surveys on which Warnock based its concept of Special Needs are rooted in approaches developed over 50 years ago. They used criteria like "dullness" and "intellectual potential" which many psychologists would now find highly questionable. Furthermore, it has also been suggested that Warnock neglected the social context of educational failure. When children make a late start at reading, they often realize they are falling behind. They begin to think of themselves as "thick" and expect less of themselves in their school work. The teacher may also lower his expectations and label them as low attainers. A vicious circle is established. Motivation falls, interest flags and the children achieve far less than they are capable of. While many staff accept the situation, a few "reach out forcefully and successfully to involve low attainers." (Brophy and Good). Where there are sufficient teachers in a school to help raise the standards of the least able over a number of years the results challenge our notions of Special Needs. Joyce Morris (1966) was one of the first researchers to notice the difference that schools can make to the attainments of poor readers. In her survey of the standards and progress in reading in Kent Primary Schools, she found that one of the best sets of results came from a school with a particularly large number of social and economic problems. She concluded that "a good deal of reading backwardness can be attributed to school conditions." In a more recent evaluation exercise, we found that in a Primary School in a North Eastern mining valley, with its pit about to be closed and a history of long term unemployment, none of the pupils were leaving with a reading age score more than eighteen months behind the child's chronological age. The Warnock Report used a cut off point of twenty eight months or more in its definitions of special need.

Critics of Warnock would argue that disability is not just intrinsic to the child. Handicap and learning difficulties could be analysed in terms of a series of factors. Attitudes towards disabled people and specific school conditions may be just as significant as the children's capabilities. (Mittler: Fraser). The physically handicapped may face additional problems because their local comprehensive is multi-storied and no lifts have been provided. Norm-referenced examinations, like the present GCE or CSE, may contribute to the poor motivation of older less able pupils because they are designed to fail a certain proportion of the population.

Initial teacher training is one of the most important ways of influencing school attitudes. The Warnock Committee considered its reform one of its "Three Areas of First Priority". All initial training courses should have a "Special Needs Element" for all students and there should be additional options for interested students to pursue their studies in greater depth. Their two major recommendations are as follows:

> A special eduation element should be included in all courses of initial training, including those leading to a post graduate certificate of education
>
> (12:7)

and:

> Those responsible for validating training courses should make the inclusion of a special needs element a condition of their approval of all initial teacher training courses.
>
> (12:11)

In retrospect, it appears that the Committee did not appreciate the resistance such proposals would run into. Pupil rolls have been falling since the late 70's, fewer Secondary teachers are required and Training Institutions are under pressure to contract or close. It is going to prove highly difficult to expand this one area and staff it satisfactorily. Many of those lecturing on P.G.C.E. courses taught in Grammar and Public schools. A minority have any interest or expertise in the field of Special Needs. The Warnock concept of a Special Needs Element represents a serious challenge to the traditional division between educational disciplines (like educational psychology and administration) and the academic subject areas (Modern Languages, Physics, Music). One of the respondents in an unpublished survey wrote:

> There is a shortage of colleagues involved presently in the P.G.C.E. who want to and are qualified to teach in this area ... It must be remembered that the P.G.C.E. has a strong subject bias.
>
> (Sewell:1983)

In many teacher training institutions it was assumed that the initial training courses were too short to accommodate such a complex field and that Special Needs would best be studied on an in-service basis. According to this argument, Special Needs was the provision of the Remedial Department or Special School. "Young teachers" should start with the great majority of average and able pupils and only when they have demonstrated competence there, would they "Specialise":

> I think I can make out a strong case for not over-emphasising Special Needs at this stage of a young teacher's career
>
> (Sewell:1983)

> We have discussed the matter at length and feel that any information put to the student body at large would be superficial and of little use at this stage of their training. It is generally believed that special educational needs as a proper study should be developed in a post experience situation
>
> (ibid)

> We do not encourage our students to undertake remedial work, which requires the expertise and experience of teaching "normal" pupils which students and probationers do not have
>
> (ibid)

Given that the D.E.S. has never seemed likely to offer a post experience programme in Special Needs to all recently trained teachers, it is difficult to see how the profession could ever be adequately prepared for teaching this large minority of pupils without some kind of initial training initiative. Furthermore, if lecturers on initial training base their courses on the suggestion that there are "normal" children who belong in the students' and probationers' classroom and others for whom remedial departments and special schools are expected to take responsibility, this will influence the way that teachers typify and treat children. In earlier research, we found that many serving teachers came back to the phrase "we weren't trained" when asked to make comments in the integration debate and Warnock.

As a teacher who had had recent promotion from a remedial post to the deputy headship of a special school put it:

> Most teachers don't want to cope and don't see it as their job. They see their job as coping with the middle of the road child. They feel they can't cope. They are not trained. (Sewell:1980)

It is scarcely surprising that before Warnock was published one of the commonest complaints by P.G.C.E. students about their courses is the lack of preparation given them for slow learners, handicapped and difficult children. The Report itself quotes a Scottish survey of newly qualified teachers: "58 per cent felt inadequately prepared for teaching slow learners." (12:5)

The Warnock Committee felt that if only small additional demands were to be placed on the P.G.C.E. timetable, teachers on initial training should be introduced to Special Needs in the "general context of .. their child development" courses. Programmes should be devised which are partly theoretical and partly practical. All teachers ought to become aware that they are likely to be concerned with children who have special needs. They ought to be able to spot some of the early signs and play a continuing part in the assessment of special needs. If, in the words of the Report, Special measures are "prescribed" they should know how to carry them out. They all ought to learn about the forms special education takes and the career structure of special education. They ought to be aware of parents' concerns and how they can be involved in the educational process. And, above all, they all ought to know where and when to refer for special help.

At a practical level, all students should be acquainted with special schools, classes and units. They ought to develop their observational skills so they can detect variations in children's learning, behaviour and circumstances. There ought to be an understanding of the practical steps necessary for meeting needs, though "this element will not be intended to equip teachers to provide specialist help", themselves. Visits, micro-teaching and videos ought to be made available to heighten skills in observation and "gain experience of special schools in a systematic way."

Such a programme is undoubtedly an improvement on much existing practice, where according to the survey cited earlier, the opportunity to study Special Needs was limited to 10 per cent of P.G.C.E. students in 44 per cent of teacher training institutions (Sewell:1983). But given recent criticisms of Warnock, we have to ask ourselves whether there might not be even more effective ways of preparing student teachers, which are more intellectually demanding and emotionally satisfactory and which provide a better match between theory and practice. Knowing about all the forms Special Education can take is obviously something that would appeal to the future administrator, but it is hardly likely to affect one's teaching on teaching practice or the probationary year. Similarly, the career structure in special education is something that only the teacher who wants to specialise will want to know about and this can be left to a post experience course. At a practical level, visits, micro-teaching and videotapes may provide a number of useful pointers, yet they are all ultimately artificial. As in carrying out measures that are "prescribed" for children with special needs, this gives too clinical a view of what actually happens in the classroom. No teacher singles out a child, examines symptoms or makes out a "prescription". The Schools Medical Officer and the Educational Psychologist may do. The teacher observes signs of special need in the course of getting to know a class, scanning them, disciplining them, listening to them and marking their books. Similarly, most of the decisions about special measures to be adopted are made by teachers in the course of termly and day to day lesson planning for the whole group. The balance between a sharp appreciation of what a child could do yesterday and what he might to today, if one "reached out forcefully", is under constant review and it is liable to updating as new topics are covered,new resources become available and classroom groupings shift.

As the Warnock Committee acknowledged, their recommendations depend on the understanding and commitment of ordinary class teachers. It would be the contention of this book that there are more realistic ways of involving student teachers in special educational provision. They can be given opportunities to get to know children with a wide range of abilities and disabilities. They can be encouraged to teach them in ways which are safe, rewarding and illuminating. And this practical experience can be used to provide a touchstone to their reading, writing and discussion of theory.

A first step might be to conceive of the preparation for teaching low attaining, handicapped and difficult children as a four to five term project, starting from the time intending teachers are interviewed for P.G.C.E. courses. Two years 'A' level work on two or three subjects and a general studies course, followed by an even more specialised three year degree course working alongside friends with very similar intellectual gifts and interests may well make for an enthusiastic and knowledgeable teacher of Sixth Formers. But they can also have the effect of making less able children or children with different experiences of life appear quite alien.

We would suggest that there are enjoyable ways for students to get to know children with the full range of abilities and disabilities in a naturalistic context, even before the first degree is finished. In many of the towns with Universities and Polytechnics there are Ph.AB. clubs where handicapped and able bodied young people can meet on equal terms. For students who enjoy sports, there are often pony trekking, canoeing or swimming expeditions, organised in all probability by the handicapped members. If one has not met disabled people before, the first experience can be rather shocking and embarrassing, but a discussion over a cup of coffee or a drink helps make one a lot less self conscious. It is often enlightening to hear about the world from the point of view of a disabled person, too.

A few special schools and local authorities

run summer camps where small groups of disabled children are integrated with able bodied children. One former student told of how the Playleader had warned the student helpers about the problems of pitying children, of being over protective and having stereotyped ideas of what they could or could not do. She had read about civil rights for disabled people and was firmly convinced of the need to let them attain independence. But until she actually worked with children in wheelchairs, she had no idea how hard it was to hold back and let them solve their own problems. One of the children in her group was fond of careering down a hillside. At the bottom of the slope was an area of loose sand. When the wheelchair came into contact with it, it stopped abruptly and threw the child out. Sue's first impulse was to rush over and help the child up. But the Playleader who had been observing both her and the child told her to let the child get back into the wheelchair on her own. Not only could she do this, she could manoeuvre the wheelchair out of the sand and back up the hill. The child had learned to do this on her own, under discreet supervision. By the end of the afternoon, she like many of the able bodied children had picked up a few bruises, but she had taken risks and the risk taking had increased her confidence, sense of well being and independence. Sue had also learned something about her own reactions to handicap, which no book or lecture could have done as graphically.

In many inner city areas, there are Play Parks run by Youth Workers to occupy children during the school holidays. Another student, Jim, described how working in a couple of these during University vacations had taught him more about discipline and control and had laid the practical foundations for his understanding of the language deprivation debate. He had been to a single sex selective school where there had only been two or three non-Anglo pupils. His home was in one of the more affluent suburbs of London, and his family had always encouraged verbal assertiveness rather than fighting or showing anger. At the first Play Park he had worked in the children only seemed to be interested in fighting. So after trying to involve them in making climbing frames or using the aerial runway, he offered to fight with them. Immediately he was surrounded by a ring of excited nine year olds, who set upon him, threw him to the ground and then dumped him in a brook.

Jim found that even though he wanted to be angry and defend himself, he could not raise his voice or even lift a hand against such tiny children. This group would not let Jim organise them, but however angry he felt inside, he could not bring himself to express it. The parental inhibitions were too strong. Every night he would go home boiling with frustration, but every morning he would return in this strange state of paralysis. Eventually the children made the mistake of confronting the other Playleaders, order was restored and Jim regained his confidence. By the end of the Easter vacation he felt he had learned more about children and the role of his own feelings in managing them.

The fact that there were other Playleaders nearby and there was always an end in sight enabled him to experiment, to relax and to learn from his mistakes.

In the Summer vacation, Jim worked in an area where a lot of the children were first or second generation immigrants from the West Indies. At first he imagined that his liberal principals made him an honorary member of the community, but to his horror he found that he could hardly understand what the children were saying. One of them kept repeating the phrase "Nunny goat" and making baaing noises. They told him later that in Jamaica, one of their favourite meals was goat curry and that they would hang long strips of goat meat in the sun and eat it dried. There seemed to be an endless supply of ethnic stories about nanny goats and nanny goat jokes and he was vaguely amused by them. It was only later that he realized that they had been referring to his own wispy beard.

Later Jim taught in a neighbouring comprehensive and he realized that this kind of verbal facility extended from the most to some of the least able children. Quite a few of the children who were in the Remedial class could talk vividly, precisely and wittily. They could not read very well, their writing was short, stilted and inconsequential, they made lots of spelling and grammatical mistakes and yet he felt that they were obviously bright and intelligent. The objective test scores made them appear as slow learners and in virtually all of their school work they functioned at a low level. Yet he felt that they just needed a little something to capture their interest and then this ability would come through. On teaching practice, he only managed to bring this out with a few children and in a few pieces of work. At the end of the probationary year, he sent me an article written for a teacher's journal comparing Freire's (1970) analysis of the way the teaching of reading is used to fail Indians in South America with the wastage of talent among inner city children. For him there was a relationship between teacher response to non-standard English dialect, low teacher expectations and poor performance. And yet he felt confident that a few individual teachers were showing the way to raising pupil aspirations.

Another student, Elizabeth, working in a similar area in a similar Play Park found that this sense of linguistic "difference" was not as strong or as intrinsic for her. She had rediscovered her enjoyment of painting and model-making. Her Playleader found some wood and they made a Punch and Judy booth. Then they made puppets out of papier mache and clothed them with remnants from a nearby dress factory. Plays were written with the children, who helped operate the puppets and a performance was put on. Working alongside the children made it easier to pick up the accent and idiom and she did not feel the sense of difference as acutely as Jim.

We could make an analogy between the way pre-school children learn about language and getting along with others through practical experience and play, and the way we should lay the foundations for teaching children with Special Needs. When we ask students to teach children with a wide range of abilities, some unable to read, others speaking a non-standard dialect, some handicapped, we could offer them more than lectures within the "general context of child development." We could enable them to prepare themselves through play and practical experiences, in places where they are not judged, where they can take risks, make mistakes and explore their own feelings.

Surveys of P.G.C.E. students' reactions to their courses often suggest that they learn much more from their Teaching Practice than from the lectures, micro-teaching, visits and videos. One of the best ways of learning about Special Needs may well be to spend one or two lessons per week in the Special Needs Department - irrespective of the main subject taught. Those who have done this seem to find this one of the most rewarding experiences of Teaching Practice, especially where there is an opportunity to discuss it with people who know the situation at school and in college. One reason for this may well be the relief that slow learners are not as difficult to teach as students are led to believe. Because group sizes are smaller, relationships between staff and pupils are more relaxed and personal. One gets to know individual children in more depth and where groups of children are taught by teams of teachers, the constant demand to keep checking on children's behaviour, to be ready to intervene, to assert oneself and play the teacher role can be a little relaxed. The student feels he can be more "natural".

Special Needs staff often appear to have a greater readiness to look beyond a given syllabus and to adapt it to what they think the children are capable of and likely to be interested in. One History teacher commented that having spent some time teaching reading in the Special Needs Department, he began to realize the problems the children in his bottom set History class would be having both with the reading level of the textbook and with some of the concepts in the course. He had been teaching Tudors and Stuarts. Having checked it with the Head of the History Department he decided to concentrate on the more dramatic stories of this time and concentrate on the Civil War. The reading lessons also made him realize that even where children were not labelled as having Special Needs, they might still be having problems reading the textbook and resource materials. There was no definite cut-off point between a "Backward Reader" and a "normal child" but the experience of looking at reading "from the bottom up" illuminated his work with a far wider range of pupils.

The Head of the Remedial Department at the author's own teaching practice school wrote to the College asking if the students who were to work there would be interested in a three day introductory course at the school. It was in a decaying inner city area with a high percentage of first generation immigrants. Truancy was rarely below 30 per cent, language problems were enormous and it was supposed that one third of the pupils left school semi-literate. Not only were there large numbers of difficult children, but the staff were demoralized by imminent threats of redundancy and school closure. According to most College criteria, this was a bad place to do a teaching practice.

The course gave the six of us on teaching practice a realistic idea of the school and as if that was not enough, pupils from the Remedial Department kept banging on the doors on the first day, demanding to have their normal lessons. And yet, alarming as the school appeared, one felt that the Remedial Department had a coherent policy, they knew where they were going, and they were relaxed enough to discuss the situation openly with us. On the first day we were shown the rudiments of the reading process through lectures, games and puzzles. Then we looked at teaching English as a foreign language. And we finished with group dynamics and its classroom applications. We learned an extra-ordinary amount in those three days - perhaps because we felt our survival depended on it - and it meant as much to us as the whole of our College based theory course.

The main subjects of the students there ranged from metalwork to history, P.E. to Social Studies and English. It was College practice to let us have fairly light timetables and we were encouraged to spend two or three of our free periods working alongside the Remedial Department. The rest of the school was as depressing as the College had predicted. Textbooks were few and out of date. Many of the older staff just seemed bewildered about what was happening to them and at lunchtimes and after school the staffroom was empty. The Remedial Department was quite different, though. On Tuesday evenings, the Head of Department gave a half hour lecture on some aspect of remedial work and as he went along he related it to children in the school. We all knew the child, we could remember what his reading was like, how he behaved in class and so on. And this brought the theory to life. Then for the second half of the session there would be a discussion about how things were going in the department, with an effort to relate this back to the theory.

Apart from the Head of Department, there were two full timers and other part timers, plus any of the students who wanted to stay after school. We got to know the other staff very well and the atmosphere in the meetings was one of trust and mutual support. If the seminar had concerned the relationship between affective development and learning, a member of the group might relate it to his own childhood experiences and how this affected his own handling of children. Problems such as the fear of one's anger or the feeling of impotence that the teacher picks up from children who fear they will never learn were freely aired.

This was an immensely exciting, although occasionally unnerving approach. One felt intuitively that working through the Teaching Practice, keeping a diary and reading the textbooks were insufficient in themselves to allow us to get the best out of our supposed "Slow Learners". What these did was to perpetuate the teaching styles of those we had been taught by. Whilst this may have been appropriate for teaching Sixth Formers or the upper streams of a Grammar School, it was a poor guide to dealing with these inner-city low attainers. Promoting more effective learning began to seem a matter of reflecting much more deeply on the realities, both in oneself and in the actual classroom.

Quite a few students, who have chosen to spend some of their teaching practice in Remedial Departments and then been enabled to examine the experience openly in school or in College, have felt very similarly about the light this has cast over the whole of the rest of their teaching. One, called Gerry, was asked to write about the relationship between his P.G.C.E. course and his probationary year for an L.E.A. magazine:

> What I miss the most is the collective exploration of our experience. I used to know that no matter how terrible and attacked I felt in wet and windy (A) I could go back to (the College) and feel that everything I felt was important, was made important by talking and writing openly and freely about what we were *actually* doing, about what was *really* happening to us.

For Gerry and many other students, there was a sense of affinity with pupils whom they felt had only a marginal position in the schools. He felt that he and many of his friends were given only partial and critical acceptance from the teaching practice schools. He felt critical and yet powerless to change much for the pupils. Learning more about how some of the low attaining pupils felt about school was one way of discovering what *really* happens. Listening to what the pupils have to say about themselves, about what happens when they are asked to read and write was a way of learning more about oneself as a teacher. Discussing this with other students who were prepared to be just as open about their own situations could make one feel at the heart of things:

> As a result, I was with people I felt very deeply about. I knew, <u>we</u> knew that we were with people we cared about. We cared for those we taught with and those we taught.

In-depth discussions about the pupils, about what happened to them in schools and what kinds of teaching approaches worked, led several of the students in Gerry's group to visit each other in their teaching practice schools. It was hard for Jane, a teacher in a successful suburban comprehensive, to imagine what teaching was like for Susanna, in a mining area, where the pit had been closed, and where a demoralised head and staff were publicly accusing each other of precipitating a breakdown in discipline. Part of the point in Jane and Susanna's visit was to:

> Sharpen their perception of variation in children's learning and behaviour and develop their awareness of variations in children's circumstances (which may give rise to difficulties in schools).
>
> (Warnock 12:8)

As one might expect, there were marked differences between their two schools in the numbers and range of children with Special Needs. But having talked so openly to one another, the main interest was in observing each other working with the pupils. Jane and Susanna had discussed what was possible, what their children seemed capable of and what got the best out of them. Now they could share their classroom with a sympathetic observer and discuss the realities of the situation fully afterwards. There was nothing artificial about the visits, both teachers were on a par and neither was in a position to give that "partial and limited" acceptance they felt that experienced schoolteachers and lecturers were giving them. No matter how painful the situation might be, there was no sense in which either student could "fail". In fact these particular peer visits turned out to be successful and illuminating for both.

Another of the Warnock recommendations which is useful so far as it goes but which could be treated more imaginatively is the use of videotapes: "in helping students to acquire skills in observation ... and see competent practitioners at work" (12:9).

It is certainly better to film successful

teachers than to interrupt their lessons with a flow of observers. This is a complex issue, however. Excellent teaching can put students off. Pupils produce different work with different teachers too and an assessment of Special Needs in one context may be of limited relevance in another. It could be more helpful to encourage some of the students to have their own teaching filmed. One can then discuss the class, the assessments made and the approaches used. Some lecturers routinely video all their students in the classroom and show the results to their peers. The ethics of doing this with Special Needs classes are even more dubious. It is bad enough knowing that one is having problems, without making them public. Situations where students and Special Needs pupils are doing something worthwhile and yet where the results are not so polished as to undermine fellow students are rare. But it is in these cases that video might be most helpful.

David's lesson with a low attaining Fourth Year group in a Tyneside Comprehensive were just such a case. He was a mature student, who had left his Jarrow Secondary Modern at fifteen to become a fitter. He had taken 'O' and 'A' levels at evening classes and his degree at the local Polytechnic. On his primary school practice he had been particulary nervous. He was awkward with the children, said he found it difficult to control the class and he had spoken very formally to them. For his main secondary practice, he had asked if he could teach in a school near where he had grown up. Many of these schools were notorious. They had tough reputations, local youth unemployment was high, there were lots of incidents of vandalism and fire damage to schools, and the large numbers of backward readers brought the proportion of children with Special Needs to about twice the national average.

One of the classes David took was a C.S.E. English Fourth Year group. By chance, I supervised another student in the same school who was teaching a non-exam Maths class. This was composed of some extremely low attaining mathematicians and disruptive children whom the teachers taking C.S.E. maths groups had demoted. Many of the children from the Maths group had asked to be put in David's group. Unlike in the primary school, where he had felt compelled to use "received pronunciation" and talk very formally, David had quickly slipped back into the idiom and accent of his youth with this group. He knew how to "have a laugh" with them, and "cap" their witticisms. His lessons really were very funny and one major critism of them was that he was so much in his element, he would not let the pupils talk or settle to writing. When we made the video, the group was reading Brendan Behan's play about the gunman who is condemned to death - "The Quare Fellow" - and the savage humour struck a chord with them. Truants were skipping Maths and coming to his lesson, and pupils who had hardly worked all year were finishing off C.S.E. essays at home for him. At one point where the class had broken up with laughter at one of David's humorous remarks about the play, he had said, "No you mustn't laugh. This is a serious play", only to set them off again. The video did not quite work as well as it could have done. One of the classroom doors was off its hinges and other children kept wandering down the corridors to have a look. Some of the wittiest children kept trying to upstage the teacher, for the benefit of the cameras. David's performance was far from faultless and he was so embarrassed by it, he only let us show the film to a very small group of friends. But one still had that unmistakeable feeling that children who had been written off as "stupid" and "hopeless" were doing something they felt worthwhile, they were producing work that was better than was expected and the classroom was alive. What was more, we could discuss with David how he had brought this off and where he planned to go from there.

Warnock does not mention the traditional P.G.C.E. Teaching Practice Diary or Long Essay as a basis for student learning about Special Needs - which is rather strange given its insistence that the inclusion of a Special Needs element be "a condition" of the validation of all initial training courses.

We found that if students who had enjoyed their "collective explorations" were allowed to adapt the written and examined elements of their course, they could learn considerably more. We had been reading Peter Abbs' "Autobiography in Education" (1978), a book that argues that education must be concerned with "the expression and clarification of individual experience". Quite a few of the students who had been working with low attaining pupils found that much of what was happening to them made much more sense in terms of their own childhood experiences:

> In the classroom I recalled memories of my childhood that I thought to be lost, momentarily seeing my lessons through the eyes of the pupil. The more I thought about this the more I realized the extent to which my attitudes towards teaching and education in general have been formulated not through any textbook learning of psychology or sociology but as a direct result of my own schooling.

This realisation first came to Mary when she was working with those who appeared to have least hope of educational success, but it became a touchstone by which to examine the experiences of the other pupils, too.

> What concerns me is that no provision is made and no alternatives are available for the pupil, who, for whatever reason will not achieve academically. Equally for the more intellectually inclined, school is frequently little more than a machine operator, putting the passive student through his mechanical paces. In either case what so often appears to be missing is an education that centres round the individual.

When Mary looked back at her own childhood, both during Teacher Practice and afterwards in the final term of the P.G.C.E. course, she realized that there were many analogies to be drawn between her own experiences and the schooling of those "for whom no provision is made". There had been teachers and children who had frightened her and made her unwilling to learn, others who made her feel "the joy of learning, the richness of experience". A "stringy uncoordinated child, nervous of heights", Mary had been made to climb a ladder and cross wall bars every week in a P.E. lesson.

> I was so afraid that my hands were always damp with sweat and I held my breath for fear of falling, every time I had to let go with one hand, moving slowly forward. One day, though, we were made to go over the top of the ladder, gripping the sides and crawling over the rungs. I can see it now and almost feel the pain in my knees as the rungs dug in. I almost froze up there, my head spinning. The teacher told me to hurry up, panicking me. I must have reached the other side. I only recall running home, proud to tell my mother.

> I find myself very angry now when I think of this. And it still happens. The child who must read aloud in the classroom, embarrassed and aware of boring the others; the child who is picked at random to write the answer to a maths problem on the blackboard, this happened to me and I saw it happen again on my first Teaching Practice.

By analogy Mary was arguing that every child has Special Needs. This is one of the strongest criticisms of the Warnock Report. Unfortunately it has also been used as a rationalisation for the lack of involvement by some College lecturers in preparing students to teach slow learners and handicapped children, as this extract for a survey questionnaire shows:

> I take it you refer to the Warnock usage of the term "Special Educational Needs", which is so extended as to be drained of meaning. All our P.G.C.E. courses are predicated on the notion of "individual needs" and are applicable to all pupils. In which case the whole P.G.C.E course is a course on Special Educational Needs.
>
> (Sewell:1983)

One could certainly endorse such a statement, if only one felt that the P.G.C.E. students on such a course felt it was "applicable to all pupils". Unfortunately, the lack of experience, understanding or interest in the pupils drawn together by Warnock among the broad majority of education lecturers makes one highly sceptical. One hopes that concerned students, teachers, advisers and H.M.I.'s press for the basic Warnock element of Special Needs lectures, micro-teaching, visits and videos. We would contend that actual play group, youth club and teaching practice experience, peer visiting and videos would be even more useful, particularly where they were supported by discussion groups with teachers who really know what happens and where these groups focused on real-life teacher-pupil interactions. There is no doubt that there is a great deal of interest among student teachers in this area and where lectures adopt a more imaginative approach that goes beyond the boundaries of the P.G.C.E. year, this enthusiasm is sustained:

> We are really delighted by the obvious interest of P.G.C.E. students in the field of special education. This interest is already evident when they join the course in the Autumn Term : I find that two thirds personally know a handicapped child or adult and that a proportion have already had some working experience with handicapped children or adults. This interest is continued through the course: the option is the most popular choice and it is quite impossible for us to provide this option to all students who request it.
>
> (Sewell:1983)

This lecturer was planning an additional non-examined Special Needs placement for after the P.G.C.E. exams:

> ... during the course of which a student would work in an auxiliary capacity in any way which suited the school or him or her. For example, some students might accompany the school camping or on special projects. The purpose of this attachment would be to enable students to get more detailed experience of the day to day work of the school, if only for two weeks in the knowledge that they were not being formally assessed.
>
> (ibid)

It is the aim of this book to suggest that working with children who all too often have a marginal role in ordinary schools can shed light on central issues like individual children's needs and effective classroom management. We would argue that despite its flaws the Warnock Report presents a useful starting point in the consideration of these children. Little is likely to improve in this grossly neglected area of our schools unless the basic recommendations on initial training are put into effect. But there are even more promising approaches which could be used where lecturers' interests and expertise permit. These approaches focus on the interaction between teachers and pupils in real classrooms, where observation and lesson planning spring from actual teaching.

The chapters that follow are designed to prepare for and build on the practical experience of working with children with Special Needs, during the teaching practice and probationary year. Whilst there are limits on the teaching of reading, writing and maths and on classroom management, we would argue that we learn most from the experience itself, through "collective explorations", peer visiting and videos or privately through our own intuitions and memories of "what really happens".

REFERENCES

Abbs, P. (1974) Autobiography in Education: Heinemann

Brophy, J.E. and Good, T.L. (1974) Teacher Student Relationships: Causes and Consequences: Holt

Clunies-Ross, L. and Wimhurst, S. (1983) The Right Balance: N.F.E.R

Fraser, B.C. (1980) The Meaning of Handicap in Children: in Child Care, Health and Development: 6:2:8J-91

Freire, P. (1970) Cultural Action for Freedom: Penguin

Mittler, P. (1975) A Handicapped Identity: Ed Borwell, D. et al: O.U

Morris, J.M. (1966) Standards and Progress in Reading: N.F.E.R

Sewell, G. (1980) Transfer to Special Schools: Unpublished MEd Dissertation: University of Birmingham

Sewell, G. (1982) Reshaping Remedial Education: Croom Helm

Sewell, G. (1983) The Warnock Report and P.G.C.E. Course: Unpublished paper delivered to ASET/DES Bretton Hall Conference

Warnock Report (1978) Special Educational Needs: Cmnd 7212 HMSO

FURTHER READING

Hannam, C., Smyth, P. and Stephenson, N. (1984) Young Teachers and Reluctant Learners: Bristol Classical Press

Hegarty, S. and Pocklington, K. (1981) Educating Children with Special Needs in the Ordinary School: N.F.E.R. Nelson

Kohl, H. (1967) 36 Children: Penguin

Mardle, G. and Walker, M. (1980) Strategies and Structure: Some Critical Notes on Teacher Socialisation: in Teacher Strategies Ed Woods, P. (1980) Croom Helm

Ryan, J. and Thomas, F. (1980) The Politics of Mental Handicap: Penguin

Thomas, D. (1982) The Experience of Handicap: Methuen

Chapter Two

SPECIAL PROVISION FOR READING

Most of the children with Special Needs are in Ordinary Schools and most of them have reading problems. One of the simplest ways of approaching Special Needs is to work with small groups of poor readers. Some lecturers now include an element of practical reading teaching in their initial training courses. This can be done before and after teaching practice by paying a regular series of visits to a given school or by setting aside part of the teaching practice timetable to teach reading in the Special Needs Department. Some lecturers, conscious of the pressure to keep their own school experience fresh and up-to-date, teach in a range of local schools. They get to know staff, pupils and materials. Where Special Needs visits can be made to the same schools, seminars can be much more precise and particularised.

Some of the most fruitful initial training seminars spring from a shared knowledge of individual pupils and given school contexts. With some initial training groups, it is possible to accommodate a number of these regular student visits in a few local schools. Each student spends a double period a week at the school. He or she works with the same pupils, doing exercises suggested by the school's Special Needs staff and hearing them read. When there is a seminar on assessment in College, the student uses one of the recommended tests with a pupil. Wherever possible tutors work alongside students and pupils, not in order to assess the student, but to enable the student to talk in greater detail about a situation with which they are both familiar. In the past this has proved difficult because Colleges have had large numbers of P.G.C.E.'s each year. As student numbers fall and College courses offer a narrower range of subject specialisations, it is becoming possible for Special Needs lecturers to work with a higher proportion of the total P.G.C.E. group.

Where quite a few students have worked in Special Needs Departments, one of the first things they notice is the variety in the numbers of children with reading difficulties between schools. In some, Special Needs provision seems quite adequate, in others it is stretched to breaking point. In some inner city schools, for instance, the Special Needs Department might be teaching a third or more of the first year intake. And yet there may also be additional children in the first year mainstream classes who seem to be having difficulties with their school textbooks. Within such a school, there may be ten or more children who are complete non-starters at the age of eleven. A suburban school in an affluent area may have very few problems, and yet it refuses to admit even those it does have. Staff from one such school explained to one student that it used to have a very small bottom stream class, which concentrated on the basic subjects, but that falling rolls have made all these special classes "unviable". A third school has special provision for 16 per cent of its pupils - the Warnock recommendation. Complete non-starters are very rare, one every five years or so. Most of its poor readers just need extra practice and after a year or two's special provision, they are fluent and accurate enough to manage the school's reading demands.

No doubt in many cases, the percentage of children deemed to have Special Needs and the proportion with very severe problems can be related to socio-economic indices like the numbers on free school meals. This was illustrated quite graphically for a student working in a Comprehensive whose catchment area had just been redrawn. Previously it had taken most of its pupils from the edges of the city's "inner ring" and its suburbs. Then it had to take a wedge of the city extending from the suburbs right into the "inner ring". The proportion of first year children with reading difficulties rose from 19 per cent to 37 per cent, according to the Special Needs Department. They also thought that the proportion of children from single parent families and whose parents were long-term unemployed had also risen dramatically. In this particular instance, the numbers of teachers allocated to Special Needs and the Departmental budget had not increased.

Special Provision for Reading

Socio-economic variables do not explain variations in numbers of pupils with Special Needs completely, however. Neighbouring schools with apparently similar catchment areas have different proportions of backward readers at intake. Some of the schools with a multiplicity of social problems seem to have higher success rates than others set in more affluent areas. The proportion of less able children entered for C.S.E. exams varies. The organization and ethos of the school and the skills of the Special Needs staff make important contributions. Two adjacent rural schools with very few serious problems estimated that they had between 10 per cent and 12 per cent with Special Needs. One school integrated all its children for most of their lessons, just making withdrawal groups for English and Maths. All were thought to read well enough for adult needs by the time they reached the end of the third year. All the children were entered for external exams. In the other school the children were segregated for the first three years for most of their lessons and in the fourth and fifth year were put in "non exam classes". Motivation and attendance were higher in the first school, whilst in the second six children left school every year with reading difficulties. Paradoxically enough, the school with the more readily identifiable special classes appeared to be less effective than the one which operated withdrawal groups only.

One of the most important controversies in Special Education at the moment is between those who believe that there are children who need a special curriculum and that this is best organized in a special class and those who believe that the labelling that accompanies special classes may do more harm than good, however well constructed their special curricula may be. In the case of these two rural schools, it could be argued that where there are few serious reading problems to start with, the children benefited from the greater stimulation of their more able peers and the higher expectations of the teachers. Given that in the more successful school, all the children could read by the end of the third year, those who had had reading difficulties could be dispersed through the option system according to interest and choice. This did not allow staff or pupils to feel that any option class was a "sink group". All pupils could benefit from an exam course. Hence the relationship between effectiveness, as judged by the speed with which children learn to read, and special provision can well turn out to be rather complex.

Variations in the provision of teacher time and materials are considerable, not withstanding. Students on a visit to a Comprehensive in a mining valley found that the Head of Department never actually taught the slow learners and that his Department consisted of two part-time redeployed primary specialists, who had no previous experience of adolescent slow learners. In other schools, the Department might consist of as many as four full timers, who devote most of their teaching time to Special Needs groups and who also liaise quite closely with a range of specialists from other departments who take a positive interest in these children.

The mining valley Comprehensive had very limited resources. All the slow learners were taught in the medical room. When a child was sick it had to endure the lesson too. When the School Nurse or Medical Officer called, the class had to move into the Staff Room. There was a single cupboard of books and most of them seemed more suited to Junior School slow learners than adolescents. There were a few reading games but they were used so regularly, all the sense of "game" had evaporated and they had been reduced to mechanical exercises. There was a single SRA programmed reading kit for the use of all the poor readers from eleven to fourteen.

In contrast, a rather better department might have a suite of rooms, with carpeted areas, armchairs and moveable desks. Books are set out in colourful displays and children invited to take books home for their parents to help them with. There may be 100 titles or more in sets varying from two to twenty. They are graded according to the age and experience of the pupils, as well as the level of reading difficulty. Card games are supplemented with audio and videotapes. There is a range of programmed material, so that pupils whose rate of learning is particularly slow experience variety and the sense of progress.

Whilst the student on a term's teaching practice is not in a very good position to make judgements on such a problem, researchers in Special Educational provision have recently had to face the problems of effectiveness and accountability. One has to ask how effectively the department teaches children to read. This is not to condone the short-comings of the very many poorly resourced

Special Needs Departments, rather to suggest that the relationship between funding and reading progress maybe rather more complex than it first appears. One very expensively resourced department might take children out of a wide range of lessons for extra reading practice, make the children feel stigmatised and so lower pupil motivation and expectation. It is not inconceivable that a department with limited full-time staffing and comparatively poor resources could involve the rest of the school's staff in helping their backward readers, thus raising their morale and so helping them more. The most important issue is how much progress the children make, not how impressively stocked the department is.

The actual resource provision of a Special Needs Department may be sustained within a well articulated and forcefully expressed departmental policy, and nowhere are arguments among Special Needs staff sharper than in what kind of emphasis they should give the various approaches to reading. Some emphasize programmed materials, to the exclusion of all else, others the analysis and remediation of each individual child's reading difficulties and some the actual practice of reading. This has been one of the sharpest controversies on Special and Remedial Education. In some parts of the country, a programmed reading scheme called DISTAR (Engelmann, Carmine and Johnson : SRA : 1978) is being used quite widely. This scheme originated in the Head Start programmes of the early 1960's. Engelmann and his associates analysed the reading process into a number of subskills or "tracks": sound-letter relationships, letter names, decoding and so on, and then redefined each subskill into hierarchies of behavioural objectives. Complex theoretical problems such as what do we mean by "reading comprehension" are thus re-assessed in terms of testable behaviour:

> The "purpose of the track" is the general curriculum objective. For example, the purpose of the track for Story Comprehension is to teach the child to focus on the meaning of the story while reading.
>
> The "behaviourial objective" is the kind of performance that can be expected from the student who has mastered the skill. For example, the behavioural objective for Story

> Comprehension is: when reading or rereading a story aloud, the student is able to answer comprehension questions when asked by the teacher.

Each stage in each of these tracks is taught, tested, revised and retested. No allowance is made for teacher initiative. One of the first letters to be taught is /M/. For the child who has difficulty memorising letter sounds, the teacher may prefer to use a range of visual cues - a picture of mountains which have a similar shape as the letter, a photograph of Mum and so on. But DISTAR just has one mnemonic:the letter shape in thick black print with a left-right arrow underneath. The children repeat the "m m m" sound after the teacher, say it as a group and repeat it individually until the teacher is sure that the child has got it. The sequence from learning letter sounds to making deductions from a reading passage is broken down into such fine detail, all of which must be followed to the letter, that DISTAR users often refer to their teachers' guides as a "Bible".

Many students and teachers feel uneasy about behaviourist approaches. They feel that something like DISTAR infringes their professional autonomy and oversimplifies the educative process. There are many educational aims which are perfectly worthwhile and yet they cannot be reduced to objective tests. Comprehension is a case in point. We have no way of knowing how another person makes sense of what he is reading. This is particularly true when children are just starting to read or else are so confused and demoralised by their past reading failures that they seem to doubt whether the words on the page are supposed to mean anything at all. Critics of "DISTAR" argue that as with other schemes, which emphasize letter-sound correspondences, the reading material is pretty meaningless anyway:

> So the robe robber went down the street. Just then a cop came up to him and said, "Stop". So the robe robber stopped.
>
> The cop said, "Can you cope with a cop?" The robber said, "How do you cope with a cop?" The cop handed a cone to the robber.

Words like "cope" and "cone" are being used to illustrate a phonetic rule, rather than to provide an engaging story, and opponents of DISTAR would argue that the ability to answer questions on such a passage had very little relevance to comprehension of literary material or an official form.

One of Engelmann's earliest colleagues, Wesley Becker (1977), would reply that compared with other approaches, tightly structured direct instructional behaviourist techniques can be shown to work with children in even the most difficult situations. The first versions of DISTAR were by far the most effective methods used in the Head Start programs. Children from deprived Inner City areas whom one would usually expect to make a very slow start in reading came in the top 10 per cent of the ability range after the First Grade and by the end of their third year they were still performing at above average levels (Becker: 1977). Gains do not appear to be linked to the simple mechanical skills like letter-sound correspondence and word recognition but to extend to tests of comprehension.

Nearly all the research done in this country suggests that children with a history of reading problems suddenly begin to progress faster than children of average ability, when they start using "DISTAR". Virtually the only note of scepticism comes in a study which the author supervised in a range of mining valley schools (Sczypka: 1981: unpublished). We found that none of the previous studies had used control groups, but had merely averaged out the scores of the children using DISTAR. In one of the schools we observed, a group of children were chosen for a DISTAR trial, extensively tested and pronounced suitable. Due to an administrative oversight, another group was picked out at the very last moment. We followed up the first group, as it received the usual mixture of phonic games, remediation of reading difficulties and reading practice from the library of Special Needs books, as well as the second group, as it was taught DISTAR. The remedial teacher herself thought that DISTAR was marvellous and that the second group were doing extremely well. We found, however, that the control, or non DISTAR group were doing better. We also found that comprehension scores were worse than mechanical skills like letter-sound correspondence and word recognition on DISTAR. And we were concerned that as pupils began to develop their reading skills to the point where they could use context cues from the passage, the banal nature of DISTAR stories could inhibit them. We would have to admit that the study was only conducted over a six-month period, that all the children were of primary age and that there was no long-term follow up. Nevertheless, we suspect that reading teachers using a wide range of resources could do at least as well, if not better than those using behaviourist approaches.

Another programme based on behaviourist principles, but often used in conjunction with other materials, is the S.R.A. Reading Laboratory Series (Parker). The children are tested and then put on a coloured card, according to their ability. Each card has a picture and a story on it. There are comprehension questions and questions on the pronunciation, spelling and meaning of words. Some cards are designed to be read at speed, to build up fluency and accuracy, others to develop note taking and reference skills. For most of the questions, very little writing is required. Alternatives are given and the pupil has to select the correct one and write down A, B or C. The overall aim of the series is to provide pupils with evidence of success. They start the program at a level where they can succeed, and progress is in such small incremental steps that very few experience failure. There are answer cards provided and pupils often mark their own work. Then they go on to the next card. The teacher's role is reduced to helping to solve the occasional difficulties, keeping the class orderly and checking the pupils' marking.

Even the most extreme opponents of behaviourism would find it hard to dispute that most children appear to enjoy the Reading Laboratory in short bursts. Unless something has gone wrong in the initial testing, most pupils get nearly all the answers right most of the time. It allows the teacher to see the individual child, while the rest get on with their work. In some schools, it has produced considerable improvements in reading en masse.

However, there are a number of problems with S.R.A. Spellings are American and some of the phonetic concepts like long and short syllables are confusing. Ward Lock have brought out a very similar package using English spelling, though some researchers have found this marginally less effective than S.R.A. (Fawcett: 1979). Whilst the S.R.A. passages are more intersting than the DISTAR stories, one doubts whether the ability to choose the correct alternative from a multiple choice question is a very reliable guide to depth of understanding.

Special Provision for Reading

Critics of the behaviourist approach to language development argue that children using such comprehension passages actually use background knowledge or irrelevant cues in question and text, without having to read the passage or understand it. They illustrate this with a set of nonsense syllables which have no meaning, but which preserves the surface paraphernalia of prose - the capital letters, punctuation marks, prepositions, articles and conjunctions and the appropriate verb and noun endings:

> Bram of Jark wicked up in the molt of Pickty. Nill macked a prommy pog. Blem nill macked mid, nill mercked a dlum muffing snick to fleck on the koddle's blem. Nill med the orkedry and blent the Plunks at the bleming of Klonk.

Questions.

1. Where did Bram grow up?
   a) Nill
   b) in the molt of Pickty
   c) Wales

2. What kind of pog did Bram mack?
   a) flerk
   b) dlum
   c) prommy

3. Where did Bram blend the Plunks?
   a) Jark
   b) Orkedry
   c) Klonk

4. Find a word meaning:

   i) twelve: ....

   ii) village ....

It is not merely carefully constructed programmed learning kits which allow pupils to get correct answers to questions on passages they do not understand. Teachers sometimes produce worksheets which are far too difficult for some of the pupils. They may all appear to be reading them and they do obtain many of the right answers, but whether they were actually drawing meaning from print is more questionable. This is particularly important for children whose reading is poor, who find much of what happens to them in school confusing and who have yet to be convinced that print is actually designed to convey meaning. Whilst DISTAR and the S.R.A. reading kits have their uses, they cannot relieve students and teachers of their responsibility to learn how children read.

Engelmann and his behaviourist colleagues would no doubt reply that we cannot ever be sure of what is happening whilst a child reads and that, providing the instructional method is properly constructed, all children would benefit from it. However, there are many remedial teachers who believe that the most effective way to teach a child with learning difficulties is to make a thorough individual diagnosis. Much of this can be accomplished through the use of objective tests. Firstly the Special Needs population is identified through screening techniques. Many comprehensives routinely use a test of reading comprehension, a Maths test and a group IQ test with the complete First Year intake. These may not provide much detailed information, but they are thought to be fairly reliable at differentiating those with Special Needs from those without. Screening school populations is often compared to the N.H.S. mass chest X-ray programme for adults. In themselves they are fairly crude instruments, but they are designed to search out cases which can then be investigated in greater depth.

The child with reading difficulties may then be given a word recognition test. Burt and Schonell are the most famous. They are lists of words in groups of five. The examiner scores each correct answer and uses the raw score to give a reading age. It is assumed that if one averaged all the raw scores of a large group whose average age was 10, then the raw score would then be equivalent to a reading age of 10. If one did the same to an older group whose average chronological age was 12, then that average raw score would be equivalent to a reading age of 12. Hence a good reader whose chronological age was 10 might have a reading age of 12 and vice versa. There are a host of practical and theoretical problems associated with this model, but since Burt and Schonell were first in the field of reading testing in this country, the notion of a reading age remains with us. In the hands of an experienced tester, the pattern of correct answers and errors can be quite revealing. One begins to form an understanding of the types of mistake this particular child might make, whether he makes letter/sound confusion, whether he reverses d/b/p, what kind of phonic knowledge he has, and occasionally some of the emotional difficulties that accompany his reading problems show themselves. For children who do not know very many words on the Burt or Schonell lists, the remedial teacher may prefer something like the Ladybird keyword list (Murray: 1969). This contains the two hundred words that are most commanly used in print. The first 12 like "the", "and" and "it" account for 25 per cent of all the words used in most pieces of writing: the first 100 account for 50 per cent.

Having formed a rough idea of what level of difficulties the child has, the remedial teacher may then employ one of the more extensive tests of phonic knowledge like Jackson (1971). Jackson has 12 tests ranging from knowledge of letter sounds and names, through simple two and three letter words to consonant blends of varying levels of difficulty and words with complex latinate prefixes and suffixes. One occasionally finds children who have clear-cut difficulties with certain well defined letter groups. These may indicate underlying linguistic problems, or that the child was absent during part of his infant schooling, and never completely grasped one of the phonics rules. One of the children who had such well defined problems had had speech problems when he grew up in Andersonstown and he had subsequently been taught by mainland teachers with very different vowel structures. Differentiating a-e-i, and learning the silent 'e' rule were especial problems for him and his early linguistic and emotional history created extra problems.

One test which attempts to give a detailed analysis of reading accuracy, phonic knowledge, pattern of errors, fluency and comprehension is Neale. A booklet with three sets of six passages is put in front of the child. The tester has a breakdown of one of the sets of passages, in which each passage is given word by word, phrase by phrase. As the child reads the passage, the tester notes down every mistake, analysing where possible whether the mistake is an omission, a reversal or whatever. The speed with which the child reads the passage is assessed and questions are asked at the end of each. There are additional questions about vision and hearing, attitudes to school and reading, on the way the child reads aloud and a simple test of phonic knowledge.

One section is about the laterality of a pupil. It has been argued (eg. Merritt) that since reading depends on the left-to-right decoding of print, underlying neurological problems may be the source of particular sequencing difficulties. Many pupils with reading problems often confuse b/d, some even m/w and t/f. They mix up was/saw, and reverse the order of words in a sentence, and letters in long words. Some remedial teachers, finding that such a child uses his right eye for reading, has a "lazy" left eye, but uses his left hand for writing, and left foot for kicking a football, would argue that his brain is receiving conflicting messages. They would then use more extensive tests of sequencing like those in the Aston Index (Newton, M.). This gives the pupils lists of numbers and sequences of symbols and drawings and asks them to reconstruct them.

Exponents of the diagnostic approach to reading difficulty would then have a range of exercises and games designed to remedy each defective skill. The letter sounds can be learned and revised through phonic games like those in Stott's kit or those sold through the Remedial Supply Company. These can be quite elaborate, with layouts like a football match or a post box. Hornsby and Shear (1976) have followed up their analysis of phonics with a set of dictations, each exercise designed to drill a particular rule. Experienced Special Needs teachers supplement these published materials with their own flashcards, games and worksheets, on the assumption that no one method will work as well for all children.

Accounts of children with reading difficulties, together with test scores and sample test sheets borrowed from local schools are often used as a way of giving students concrete examples of the complexities of reading difficulty. They may well show the interplay of handicapping conditions, like poor sight or hearing, supposed underlying neurological problems, social and emotional difficulties and IQ with given reading skills and deficits. Terence, for instance, was partially sighted. He had nystagmus, which is a neurological problem associated with rapid involuntary movements of the eyeball. He also had a squint and was long sighted. He used his right eye predominantly, but was left handed. His speech, hearing and motor skills were fine. The partial sightedness was familial and his mother and maternal grandfather had done reasonably well in spite of it. His IQ was slightly above average. Terence had been sent to a unit for partially sighted children and later a residential special school, but his mother had always hoped he would attend an ordinary school. At eleven he had joined an ordinary comprehensive, but no special tuition was allowed him. His basic skills had regressed until at the age of 14 years and 3 months, he had gained a reading age of 6 years and 8 months on the Schonell Word Recognition Test. Of the first hundred Ladybird Key words, Terence had recognised 86. He knew 24 of his letter sounds, he confused vowel sounds and identified only 15 out of the 50 initial consonant blends on the Jackson Test PS7. Errors on this test indicated problems in sequencing and b/d and t/f reversal.

Students discussing such a case history would no doubt realize that since Terence had an average IQ and his sight was good enough for him to read so many of the Ladybird Key words, there is no reason that he could not be enabled to make speedy progress. He needs to be taught the remaining letter sounds and the consonant blends. He needs to differentiate b/d and t/f: and if he learns sufficient of the phonic rules he should be able to analyse words into phonic clusters and overcome the sequencing problems. It might be necessary to find him reading books with especially large print, and the nearest unit for partially sighted children might be of help.

Such discussions can be very stimulating. Recently, however, many of the assumptions behind the diagnostic approach have been questioned. Firstly, it is argued that the causes of a reading problem are not always the best guide as to treatment. In other words, Terence might be partially sighted, 14 and have a reading age of 6 years 8 months , whilst David has a long history of truancy is 13 and has a reading age of 7 years 1 month. Despite the difference in aetiology, however, their tuition will be similar. Secondly, it is argued that quite a few successful readers display very similar types of error to those with difficulties. Clark (1970) and others have argued that mixed laterality is a feature of many children and that a child may only learn to sequence data on a left to right basis <u>as</u> he learns to read. Correct sequencing is something that develops in most children as they grasp the reading process.

For some Special Needs teachers, however, the strongest criticism of the diagnostic approach is that it turns the poor reader into a "case", and the reading process into a set of problems. They would argue that the last thing a backward reader needs is to be treated as a kind of medical specimen. Reading ability is a continuum, which extends from the child who has difficulty with "and", "the" and "but" to the well educated adult. This group could well be referred to as using the "language experience" approach. They would argue that whilst there are pieces of phonic knowledge that some readers are unaware of, most of them have been taught most of the basic rules already in primary schools; and the commonest problem for the secondary Special Needs teacher is not ignorance of reading skills but confusion. According to the language experience group, backward readers need to find strategies to use the phonic skills, the background information and the contextual clues they have, in order to work out what the words mean. They would say that the diagnostic approach treats the pupil as an object to be analysed and drilled, whilst they see the pupil as a subject, who is attempting to derive meaning from print.

"Language experience" resources will look quite different from those of the DISTAR user or the diagnostic remedial teacher. Many of the reading materials will be generated by the children themselves. Even the very weakest reader will have his own "dictated experience" stories, which he may have told the teacher, who then has them printed and illustrated. Gavin, for instance was a fourteen year old boy who could read his own name, about a dozen words and most of the single letter sounds. He found it very difficult to put a three letter word together, if he did not already know it as a whole, and even when he succeeded in reading the simplest words it cost him terrible effort and concentration. He might learn a word, then came across the same word five minutes later and not be able to recognise it again.

Gavin had been given programme courses in phonics, his particular problems had been analysed and "treated", but he lacked any sense of reading as something that meant anything to him. So after establishing rapport with a "language experience" teacher, he was persuaded to tell a story about what had happened to him in a local disco. He had been threatened, and when he had refused to hand over his money, he had been set upon by six of the boy's mates. The next day he saw the same boy on a bus while he was with his own mates. They had followed Gavin's enemy and wreaked their revenge. The teacher made rough notes of the story, then had written it, excising most of the long words and using very short lines and paragraphs to emphasise phrases and twists in the plot. Overall, the teacher had attempted to keep as close as he could to the rhythm and phrasing of Gavin's speech, so that as he read his own story, they would mean something to him:

> So six lads
> came up.
> They did Gavin over.
> They fixed him.
>
> But Gavin did not cry.
> He will get them back.

One of the Art teachers in the school was asked to illustrate the text. The drawing on the page opposite the section quoted above shows six skin heads, each one numbered one to six. When Gavin tells the skin heads to get lost he says, "I am not a mug". The cartoonist drew a picture of a coffee mug with Gavin's face on it. Some local authorities or teachers' centres will paste the typescript and drawings up, "print" them on a photocopier and bind the whole production up in its own cover. The purpose would be to show the individual pupil that books could relate to their experience and be enjoyable to read. Some experienced Special Needs teachers have collections of stories, pupil joke books, magazines and projects written for and by backward readers.

Despite the success of programmed materials like DISTAR with experienced teachers, it could be argued that for a subject teacher to be allowed to spend a lesson a week, in the Special Needs Department of a Comprehensive, talking with a small group of poor readers, getting them to tell him their stories and reading them back to him, could not only provide them with an additional bit of encouragement, but could also help the teacher to learn more about the culture and language of the area and the interests of the children. In the desolate mining areas of the North East, the stories may well be set round the allotments where the pigeons are kept, or "crees":

> I have a brother
> My brother lets me

get on
his bike.
The Bike is
a Suzuki 100 T.S.

I have to
clean it.
Then he says
I can have it
down the crees.

The effort involved in getting close enough to the children to get them to tell one their own stories is more than repaid in terms of the insight it gives and the amount of work they put into their own reading and writing. Mutual understanding is essential to the language experience approach. Many failed readers find the business of concentrating on subskill exercises lesson after lesson stultifying and frustrating. It helps if they feel the teacher is involved. In order to provide the children with strategies they can use in their reading, the teacher has to understand how the children piece together the meaning of a text. The way that a child reads the text becomes a "window" on the child's reading strategies (Bullock Report 1975). Making tapes of children reading and then discussing them with one's tutor and fellow students can be another way of shedding light on learning difficulties and the teaching process.

The pupil in the following transcript is a fifteen year old boy called Trevor. At the time when it was made, his reading age had risen to 8.2 : that is, his reading ability was that of an average first year Junior School child. When I had begun to see him his reading age was 7, and through using books, that he had chosen or dictated, he had made a years progress in just over a term. Trevor had been deeply confused when I first met him. He frequently went into a blind panic when he encountered a new or difficult word, or simply when his concentration ran out. For a term we had discussed what was good in his reading, what happened when he lost concentration, how he must go back and check a word if it sounded wrong. He knew that if he got really stuck, I would always help him out. But he also knew he had to take risks, try to break words down or guess in context. It did not matter if he made mistakes. The important thing was to realise that when he made an error, the passage would not make sense. And when the passage sounded wrong, he must find out why. The book that Trevor had chosen in this extract was "In History: Flight" (Smith and Newton: 1971) and this is what he was trying to read:

> There are other legends of Eastern Kings who had large baskets which were pulled through the air by large birds. There are also many records of men who jumped from high towers with bat-like wings strapped to their arms. Many of these men were killed and even those who were not killed did not really fly.
>
> Though flying began only in the twentieth century, for hundreds of years men had weapons and toys which used the principles of flight. The arrow had feathers to give it balance during flight. The boomerang's curved shape helped it glide through the air.

This is how Trevor read it with my help:

Pupil: There are other legends of .. Eas...

Teacher: Now how are you going to check it out?

Pupil: Split it up ... Eastern kings who were pulled through the air by large birds. There are also many .. records .. of men who jum...ped

Teacher: Jumped .. yes.

Pupil: From high towers with large bat .. like .. wings s.. supple .. supposed to

Teacher: Check that one.

Pupil: Strapped to their arms. Many of the men were killed and even those who were not killed did not really fly. Through (sic) flying really began only in the twentieth century, for hundreds of years men had .. weapons ..

Teacher: Good.

Pupil: And toys which used the principles of flight. The arrow had flights to give it balance during flight

Teacher: Good. Do you want to carry on?

Pupil: The boomer.. burming.. d

Teacher: No, "boom" was right. How does it go after that?

Pupil: Boomerang.

Teacher: Very good.

Pupil: Carried

Teacher: Check.

Pupil: Carved sharp

Teacher: Now how are you going to split that one?

Pupil: Curved shape helped it glide through the air.

By this stage, Trevor's reading is characterised by periods of confidence and fluency, where his understanding of the book carries him through long and unfamiliar words accurately and without hesitation:

> toys which used the principle of flight

but these are interspersed by confusion and error. With just a slight reminder he could work out difficult individual words like "Eastern .. records .. weapons" but unusual phrases unsettle him "bat-like wings strapped.. The boomerang's curved shape". The individual words could now be analysed and sounded out, but the phrases themselves do not appear to mean much to Trevor. So when he gets to the word "strapped" he begins to guess wildly, and his reading almost broke down altogether in the last sentence.

Despite Trevor's continuing problems, it is quite clear that he is using his understanding of the meaning of the book, to help him analyse or recognise words, just as his grasp of the words and phrases helps to shape his understanding of the book. This in itself represents a crucial development in Trevor's reading. When I first started teachng him, he seemed to lunge at words and phrases with something close to panic. It was often necessary to stop him reading, calm him down, talk about the content of the book with him and then begin again. His concentration span was less than a minute and even with these frequent breaks he would be utterly exhausted after twenty minutes.

One of these continuing problems seems to have been caused by faulty eye movements, but where these brought about errors which still made sense within the overall context of the passage, there was no attempt to intervene. Towards the end of this section Trevor repeats the word flight:

> The arrow had flights (instead of "feathers") to give it balance during flight.

The word "flights" is often used to mean the feathers of an arrow, and Trevor had probably inadvertantly picked it out from the line above and the line below, where it was also used. Presumably he had not internalised the convention that writers do not use the same word twice in a sentence and it is tempting for the teacher to intervene. Indeed many remedial teachers who accept the notion of specific dyslexia might see it as a priority to correct perceptual errors of this kind. They would argue that there is a quite clearly defined group of backward readers who persistently confuse the up/down, left/right sequencing of reading. They reverse the order of words in sentences, they reverse letters in words (was/saw) and they misread the reversible letters and numbers : t/f: n/u: m/w: b/d/p: 2/5: 6/9.

Some recent research suggests that some of these children with specific dyslexia take longer to read nonsense syllables and differentiate correct and incorrect spellings. Other psychologists find no such clear differences between poor readers with high IQs and poor readers with low IQs, or between dyslexics with low reading scores and younger children of average intelligence with the same reading scores (Frith). The argument is a complex one and our understanding of the causes of such perceptual errors is still uncertain. The problem for the practical teacher, however, is that where children with reading difficulties are ignored or badly taught, perceptual errors can impede the search for meaning. This particular pupil, Trevor, had been rehearsed in the differences between though, through and although, but as this had always been done outside the reading context, he had merely ended up confused. The actual meanings of the separate words had been lost in a kind of semantic porridge. So when he had said:

> Through flying really began only in the twentieth century

There was little point either correcting him or getting him to check the word out.

Teaching Trevor was becoming a matter of getting him to "check out" what sounded wrong to him. This meant that he had to have the confidence to admit to himself and his teacher that he could make a mistake. Yet reading errors had all kinds of alarming and depressing connotations to him and even at this stage one felt he was never far from panic. When confronted with a word he neither recognised or anticipated, like "boomerang", he gave wilder and wilder guesses, which culminated in b/d reversal. This word conveys little to him and the phrase of which it is a part gives no clues to its meaning or to what the rest of the sentence is about. It seems to cast a shadow over his reading. Where previously this would have meant that the teacher would have had to break off, explain what a boomerang looked like, draw a picture of one and so on, Trevor is now confident enough to pick up the thread again and resume his reading.

It is often argued that the process of reading is ultimately a form of thinking and that for a teacher to help a child with reading is to monitor what the passage means to the child. In the case of backward readers with a history of learning difficulties, it is just as important to understand how the child _feels_ as he reads, as well. The use of the language experience approach with poor readers, as opposed to the use of a programmed instructional kit, means that the teacher has to calm the pupil, get him to make light of his problems and in the last resort help him with a word or a phrase. At the same time, one is trying to understand what the pupil is making of the passage. In this instance Trevor appears not to understand the significance of "bat-like wings strapped to his back". The teacher has to work out how much help and reassurance the pupil needs to read the words accurately and how important an understanding of that phrase is to the whole book.

This section of the paragraph was badly written and the actual shape of the wings did not matter very much. But the boomerang's "curved shape" was of more relevance. Trevor was interested in planes. This is why he had chosen the book, and he already knew something of the principles of flight. He knew about delta wings and the importance of shape in wing design. And where other boys might have got more out of a dictated experience story or a piece of fiction, he was fascinated by planes.

Trevor made remarkable progress. His reading age rose by a year in two terms. One could see that his fascination with the subject and his understanding of it enabled him to read longer and larger passages without hesitation. His grasp of the so called "building blocks" of reading - the basic phonics, and the ability to sound out larger words - was growing. One would not argue that certain children who have never been taught the basics would not benefit from a highly structured programme, either diagnostically based or like DISTAR, or that periodic revision of the "building blocks" will not benefit readers like Trevor.

Teachers of reading should always have long term plans involving recognition of letters, letter clusters, syllables and so on, with a range of written exercises, spelling lists and dictations to reinforce those that certain children find tricky. But to the exponents of the language experience approach, such exercises should be secondary to the fostering of the search for meaning.

After a couple more years of effective teaching it might have been possible for Trevor to have reached the stage that the next extract illustrates. This is a tape transcript of a boy who was younger than Trevor, but who had a reading age of 10.5 and was just about ready to join full-time mainstream English sets. He had made considerable strides in the first two years of the Secondary School and his reading is not unlike that of an adult. Here he is reading an extract from "Walkabout", an easy read version by Nobes (1982). The few mistakes are underlined.

Pupil: The two children were along..alone in the vast Austrialian desert.
Teacher: Good.
Pupil: They were afraid and they clung together, their backs against <u>the</u> rock.
Teacher: Good.
Pupil: Far below them a little stream ran..down .. the bed of the gully.
Teacher: Good.
Pupil: There was no moon. It was dark and quiet. The boy moved closer to his sister. She held his hand tight and whispered "All right, Peter I'm here".

Teacher: Well done

Pupil: She felt him... she felt him relax a little and he stopped shaking. When a boy is only eight, *his* big .. a big sister of 13 can be a great comfort.

Teacher: Good.

Pupil: "Mary" he whispered, "I'm hungry. Lets have something to eat. The girl took a stick of barley sugar from the pocket in her dress. It was their last one. She broke it and gave him half. She put the other half back in her pocket. "Don't bite," she whispered. "Suck". They did not know *where* .. why they were whispering.

Teacher: Excellent.

Pupil: Perhaps it was because everything was so quiet, like in a church. Or perhaps it was because they were afraid. The boy finished his barley sugar sweet and began to fidget. "Aren't you comfortable, *Peter*" she asked.

Despite the comparative ease of the passage, Alan was nervous of the tape recorder and needed a lot of reassurance. He made five mistakes in just under two hundred words but this is not unusual for adult readers. He corrected along/alone and where/why himself, presumably because the word does not make sense in the context of the rest of the sentence. "his big sister" might just have been allowed to stand for "a big sister", but by this stage in his reading development Alan has developed the adult trick of picking up two or three words at a time by sweeping forward along the line; then, whilst these next two or three words are held in the short term memory store, his eye sweeps back over the words he has just spoken to give himself a visual check. These scanning and checking eye movements form a complex pattern, quite different from those of the confused and more backward reader like Trevor. Alan still makes a few trivial errors ("Peter" for "Pete": "the" for "a") but he has now fully internalised the range of mental processes and feedback "checks" that we earlier saw Trevor learning. The passage is read accurately, fluently and, once Alan has got beyond the first three sentences, with apparent understanding.

The only problems that Alan has are in this short introduction:

The two children were alone in the vast

> Australian desert. They were afraid and they clung together, their backs against a rock. Far below them a little stream ran down the bed of the gully.

There was a relatively long pause between "ran" and "down" and another between "down" and "the". What seems to be happening is that Alan is scanning the end of the sentence whilst he is reading the middle of the sentence out loud. He glimpses the words "bed" and "gully". "Bed" cannot mean something you sleep in, because it has a stream running through it. "Gully" is unfamiliar, and Alan has to check back in his long term memory store to see whether he knows the word and whether it fits in the rest of the sentence. If his reading had been a little less advanced, the teacher might have let him get to the end of the sentence, then have a short discussion about what these two words mean, where Pete and Mary had found themselves and what the area looked like. The problem is not a linguistic one - as in the construction that almost defeated Trevor, "but - like wings strapped" - so much as conceptual. What is a gully? What would the streams in the Australian desert look like? The answers to these questions depend on general knowledge more than reading skill, and whether Alan understands fully the phrase or not, he reads it with aplomb. With this degree of reading competence, Alan will probably be equal to many of the reading demands of adult and school life and he is ready to leave the special needs group.

This is not to say, that taught by an informed English teacher, his reading could not continue to develop. In the past, there has been a tendency to see a considerable divide between those with special needs and those in mainstream groups and to assume that once a pupil has been "promoted" he is capable of tackling and learning from everything the more able pupils read. The most able readers in the Special Needs groups are often better than the least able in the mainstream, and the books that these less able children are given are quite unsuitable. This was borne out very clearly in a Midlands school in which I had helped to set up a scheme where teachers from a range of subject departments had been trained in the language experience approach. The less able mainstream second year children had been divided between one experienced English teacher who had never worked in a Special Needs Department and a less experienced

English teacher who had. The first gave his group books from the English stock cupboard which were too difficult for all but the most able readers in his class. Reading lessons were virtually silent and comprehension was dealt with in separate lessons with special exercises from a Course book. The second gave her group a mixture of books from the English and Special Needs Departments. She did a fair amount of play reading to build up fluency and confidence. And comprehension was mainly developed by following up difficult passages in the books that the class was actually reading with class discussion. When the second years' reading was tested at the end of the year, the first group had made three months progress, the second a year and a month.

Easy reading books like "Walkabout" often follow the original quite closely. With wide ranging bottom sets or with mixed ability groups which include poor readers, one can use both versions. It is relatively straightforward to suggest that pupils with reading difficulties use the easier version, if one has up to date reading scores and if one has tested the readability level of the books. Some schools still only test the reading of those whom they suspect of having a problem and only measure the reading demands of the books in the Special Needs Departments. Whilst it is probably too much to ask a student on teaching practice to test all the children in his or her own Special Needs groups, it can be illuminating to try out one or two of the most common tests with very small numbers of children. Not only does the practical experience help teachers "sharpen their perceptions of variations in children's learning". (Warnock) It also enables one to grasp the strengths and weaknesses of so-called objective tests.

The most widely used is still probably F.J. Schonell's Word Recognition Test. This is often used to screen large numbers of children for learning difficulties, even though others are easier to administer, and as we have seen, in the hands of an experienced teacher, it can provide diagnostic clues. Critics of word recognition tests have argued that reading is much more than reading words out of context. Some children whose understanding of what they read is demonstrably sound but who make lots of mistakes when reading aloud do badly on this kind of test. Others who are very methodical but whose comprehension may be weak can do well. Schonell clearly realized this. It is perhaps the use to which teachers put his test rather than the test itself that we should criticize. However, it has only become clear in the last 10 years that changes in language use affect competence in reading quite markedly. The ability to recognize particular words on a word list depends to a certain extent on the frequency with which words are used and this alters with changes in the media, fashion and technology. The word "refrigerator" was seen as quite difficult when these tests were devised, whereas "gnome" and "canary" were relatively easy. "Terrestrial" proved one of the most difficult words on Schonell's word list to generations of pupils, until Speilburg made his film 'E.T.' There is something inescapably arbitrary about any list of words and the account Schonell has given us of the way his Test was validated is neither detailed nor statistically sophisticated. When Cyril Burt's Word Recognition Test was recently reorganized and recalibrated, it was given a Standard Error, that is an index of its statistical reliability, for the first time. It became obvious that at both ends of range of reading competence, the test was relatively unreliable. It also became clear that difference scores of three months or so were not to be used with any confidence, either. Yet, not only do large numbers of Special Needs teachers still prefer the old versions of these tests, they use their assessments of short term reading progress to decide which children have Special Needs and which should be "promoted".

One of the author's students tested a group of Junior school children on the modern versions of Burt and Schonell at the beginning and end of a teaching practice. Not only did the average difference between the two tests' scores almost equal the amount of progress each test indicated the children had made: with two children out of the twelve the difference between the two tests' scores was greater than a year. Some Special Needs teachers persist in assuming that the reading age is something that resides in the child, like the mental age which supposedly reflects the "genotype" of the child's intelligence. Careful use of the tests should make obvious what crude instruments they are and how much more sceptical the well informed teacher should be about labels like "Backwardness" and "Special Needs".

Differences can be even more marked when we

compare tests constructed on two different principles. The G.A.P. and Gapadol, use passages of varying difficulty for silent reading. Every so often there is a word missing from the text. Using their understanding of the context, their ability to scan ahead and check back, the children have to guess the missing words. This should indicate an understanding of the reading process, and provide a more broadly based assessment of reading competence than the ability to recognize individual words out of context. There are a number of problems with the use of this Cloze technique in group tests, some of which the constructors of these two recognize, and some of which they do not. Firstly, it is much easier to cheat in a group written exam than on an individual test. There are parallel versions printed on different coloured paper which virtually eliminate cheating, so long as the children's desks are set in serried ranks, all facing the front. It is no help, however, where pupils sit at nests of tables. One needs the reading skill of an average eight year old to be able to anticipate missing words, so the thresholds of these tests are high. This means that some poor readers with a poor sense of self esteem and a high expectation of failure lose heart and find the test extremely threatening.

Another technical problem is that Gapadol was recently reprinted in quite a different way, without being restandardized. Previous versions of the test had a corresponding number of dashes for each letter in the missing words. Now it has an unbroken line. In some instances this made an average of well over one year to group scores, considerably increasing the numbers of pupils with "Special Needs". No doubt this kind of problem is easily dealt with but it is a sharp reminder that even with the most sophisticated objective reading tests, one must beware of too great a reliance on reading scores. They do not relieve the teacher of the responsibility to make his or her own observations. One needs to know which test was used, what it attempts to measure, what are its limitations both practical and statistical, and, even more important, how well it squares with informal observations made in the actual teaching context.

When many experienced Special Needs teachers take over a group, they allow the pupils some time to settle down, then give them formal tests. All this time, however, they are making detailed observations of the group and of the reading skills of the individuals within it. Teachers listen to them reading in a variety of different contexts - in plays and stories, on their own and within a group, making notes of what the child can and cannot do, the hesitations and general patterns of errors. With some pupils there may be comments on the whole range of reading subskills: basic phonics, the ability to analyse words into syllables, the ability to sound out long words and guess in context; with others, particular problems may predominate: omitting words, carelessness about word endings. With most there will be notes on pupil attitudes to the reading process. An entry from one teacher's notebook about Alan, the boy whose reading of "Walkabout" we looked at earlier, taken from the first fortnight of term, reads as follows:

Alan : R.A. 9.8. G.A.P. July 19__

Ring of Bright Water : Readability level 9 +
wear = wore
I would love = it would (self correct)
passes = pass
(hesitant : omitted line: did not realize he had skipped a page)
though = they
(picking up on self correct : 95% - 96%)

Since this is the beginning of a school year, one would expect many poor readers to make a larger number of random errors than usual, so not all are noted. Typical errors, though, are verb tenses (wear = wore : passes = pass). He misreads whole phrases. His fluency is rather poor, he has not developed the checking and scanning skills he had by the end of the year, otherwise he would have noticed these omissions, especially that of the whole line. The last percentage figures indicate that in a passage which the teacher had picked out as typical of the book. Alan had made first 5, then 4 errors in 100 words. Since the average adult often reads at 97% accuracy and 95% is reckoned to be sufficient for comprehension, we see that Alan is coping quite well with a book of this difficulty, considering it is the beginning of term.

For pupils who have a positive view of their reading but who make silly mistakes and fail to check them out, it may be useful to tell them they have an accuracy rate of 96%. Once rapport has been established with a group it may be possible to play games which encourage accuracy. One can see how many lines they can read without a mistake, or how many mistakes they make in 20 lines. With younger pupils one can put a chart up in the reading room to show progress, with older ones one can offer a prize. Accuracy can become an obsession for both pupil and teacher and one has to remember that one's primary aim, the ability to read for meaning, can be accomplished even while one makes mistakes. Nevertheless if one has reached rather a dull patch in an otherwise engaging novel, this can help to keep up the high levels of concentration one needs.

Some writers on curriculum objectives for pupils with Special Needs refer to "processual objectives" (Brennan: 1979) and it is the ability to create a quiet, purposeful atmosphere, where all the pupils know how important learning to read is and where they are concentrating as hard as they can which is the main aim of the language experience teacher. One is not instructing them in a series of reading sub-skills, as with DISTAR. One is not diagnosing difficulties and giving them exercises, games and kits to enable them to overcome them. One is listening carefully to what the pupils read, creating a degree of rapport and commitment where pupils and teachers work together on analysing the pupils' approaches and helping them to find strategies which are successful. This may sound too much to ask of a student teacher. Notes made on a teaching practice may miss some of the more complex patterns in the way pupils make sense of a text. But the assessment of learning difficulties must be judged in terms of the teaching effectiveness. Pupils will often work harder for someone new, particularly if they feel the teacher is interested in them. The degree of commitment may be at least as significant as the thoroughness of the analysis.

Ultimately one's purpose is to ensure that as many of the children with Special Needs learn to read as well and as quickly as possible. Not only is life harder for secondary school pupils who cannot read, teachers in the wider curriculum may find them more difficult to motivate. In many schools, small groups of non-readers leave every year to face additional problems in the world of work. In deprived areas, the proportion of non-readers can be alarmingly high. Much of this is unnecessary. If there is a range of subject staff who have worked with Special Needs on their reading and who can follow up the work of the Special Needs Department, one can have a situation where all the pupils can leave with reading ages over 11, able to read a daily paper, fill in forms and cope with most of the written information on which survival in a modern society depends.

In well organized schools, it is quite possible for pupils who left primary schools with quite marked reading difficulties to reach the fifth year reading as fluently and with as great an understanding of print as pupils who never had such problems. Very few schools test children's reading as they leave. They are only accountable for pupil's exam results, not for their success in the skill that underpins all academic achievement. Perhaps with the introduction of pupil profiles this might change. But it should be obvious to any student or probationary teacher who works with low ability fourth or fifth year pupils how effective their school's special provision is by hearing these children read.

REFERENCES

Becker, W.C. (1977) Teaching Reading and Language to the Disadvantaged : Harvard Ed Review: 47:4

Brennan, W.K. (1979) Curricular Needs of Slow Learners : Evans Methuen

Bullock Report (1975) A Language for Life : HMSO

Clark, M.M. (1970) Reading Difficulties in Schools: Penguin

Engelmann, Carmine and Johnson (1978) DISTAR

Frith, U. (1980) Cognitive Processes in Spelling : Academic Press

Fry, E. (1977) Fry's Readability Graph : Journal of Reading : 242-252

Goodman, K.S. (1982) Language and Literacy : Routledge and Kegan Paul

Hornsby, B. and Shear, F. (1976) : Alpha to Omega : Heinemann

Jackson (1971) Get Reading Right : Robert Gibson

Merritt, J.E. (1971) Reading Failure : A Re-examination : in Reading: Problems and Practices : Ed Reid, J.F. Ward Lock

Murray, W. (1969) Teaching Reading : Ladybird Books

Neale, M.D. (1958) Neale Analysis of Reading : MacMillan

Newton, M.J. (1979) : Aston Index : L.D.A.

Nobes, J. (1982) Walkabout : Hutchinson

Parker, D.H. (1963) SRA Reading Laboratories

Schonell, F.J. (1942) Backwardness in the Basic Subjects : Oliver and Boyd

Sczypka, C. (1981) DISTAR an evaluation : Unpublished B. Ed Dissertation : University of Durham

Sewell, G. (1982) Reshaping Remedial Education

Smith and Newton (1971) In History : Flight : MacDonald

Stott, D.H. (1964) Programmed Reading Kit : W & R Holmes

Chapter Three

TALKING AND LISTENING : A PROBLEM OF CONTROL

Shortly after the Liverpool riots of 1981, I was invited to visit an E.S.N. (M) school just outside Toxteth. The L.E.A. had plans to develop the school as a Special Education resource centre for the area, with in-service workshops for local teachers and short term coaching in the basic skills for low attainers from neighbouring comprehensives. The atmosphere in the school was orderly and calm. There were eye catching displays on all the corridors, with pupil writing of a high quality. What was particularly striking, however was the amount and kind of pupil talk. This was the fast, witty, competitive talk of inner urban adolescents.

On closer inspection, it appeared that the children were being encouraged to think out loud, as an accompaniment to practical activities, reading, writing and maths. At clearing up time in the motor mechanics class for the leavers, there was hardly a pause in the conversation. Yet the teacher orchestrated this talk in such a way that speakers were given time to think and everyone else in the class was expected to listen. Such levels of class participation are rare enough with any groups of school leavers, and it represented the reverse of what many teachers expect from classes of children with Special Needs: there was a lot of talk but very little noise.

Watching children in special schools or in the Special Needs Departments of ordinary schools talking and listening to each other and their teachers can make the job look easy. Both class and teacher appear so natural, the discipline so subtle as to be almost non-existent. Yet for most of the teachers who believe pupil-talk to be an essential part in the learning process, such relationships have to be worked for. Even in this Liverpool school, there was one class where the atmosphere was quite different. It was colder and more muted. The pupils were orderly, and the classroom well organized but the vigour of the rest of the school was absent. An experienced supply teacher was in charge. Despite the fact that the children were used to a lot of talk, she did not know them well enough and she felt she had to keep her distance.

All pupil talk can appear overwhelming to the solitary teacher, but the talk of less able pupils can affect even experienced teachers in a peculiar way. Quite a few teachers seem to equate the good teacher of Special Needs classes with tough discipline and the ability to "keep them quiet". According to such a view, it is better to set "busywork" like copying, drawing or doing exercises which can be carried out in silence, than to get the children to talk and listen to each other. In one school where we were doing some research on the relationship between teacher-pupil attitudes and pupil attainments, many of the staff thought that the best teacher of low attainers was a Mr Grey, whilst virtually all the slow learners thought he was their worst. Mr Grey would explain the topic of the lesson to the class, then he got them to write in silence for the rest of the time. The pupils did not mind that he was strict. They appreciated the fact that if they finished their work early, he would let them relax. If they had worked hard all week he would take them to the video room for half an hour on a Friday afternoon. What the pupils objected to was that he would never explain things "properly". He saw his job as teaching the topic. But he would never question the class to see if they had understood. He would never discuss the work with them individually. If they were "stuck" they knew better than to ask for help. The pupils felt he was not interested in what they made of his lessons. There was no real point of contact. They felt as if they were not learning very much and that Mr Grey was not treating them like "human beings". If one put to the children that many of their teachers thought Mr Grey's discipline was good, they would have agreed. But they preferred teachers who could "go a bit mad if we come into the lesson laughing or being silly" but who could also "have a joke" with them and "have a lot of patience and take time with us to get us through hard work".

Giving pupils, who have difficulties with words and ideas, time to explain what they think, and getting the rest of the class to listen to them can do a great deal to involve pupils in the lesson. For those who feel that they are failures so far as school is concerned, this can make them feel that they themselves and their ideas are important. A class where the teacher can make all the children listen in an active way whilst first one, then another tries to put his thoughts into words can raise the esteem of the actual speakers and make the whole class feel respected. In Barry Hines' novel 'A Kestrel for a Knave", there is a classroom scene where Billy, a boy who "has a job to read and write", is persuaded to talk about his grand passion - his Kestrel. Billy is always getting into trouble, for not paying attention in school, for fighting and for thieving. His friends tease him because he is small and poor and fatherless. When Mr Farthing, his English teacher, tries to get him to join in a class discussion, he feels he has nothing to say. When eventually he is persuaded to tell the class about "Kes", they fall quiet, impressed with his knowledge and skill and momentarily lost in respect for him as a person.

The moment soon passes. Billy is in his last year at school and though Mr Farthing visits Billy to watch him flying the Hawk, he does not do much more to build on this lesson. Yet for many of the pupils who are "odd" or "different" or who find reading and writing difficult, the discovery that they can command the attention of their teachers and their peers can provide a way of overcoming low expectations. Michael, for instance, had learned to speak late. He had undergone speech therapy and he had a residual stammer. He had only learned to read in the first year of the Secondary School. He had found writing difficult, his spelling was poor and his sense of sentence structure very weak. He had a low opinion of his abilities and because of his residual stammer he liked to pass unnoticed by his teachers. The two things he was really interested in were farming and horse racing. Eventually he joined a mixed ability City and Guilds group, taking the Agricultural Foundation course. Some pupils were also entered for a few 'O' levels, most for a few C.S.E.s whilst the weakest, like Michael, were felt unlikely to pass any exams at all.

We lived in a town where there was a race-course and in one of our English lessons, we read Philip Larkin's poem about retired racehorses, "At Grass". I asked the class what it described and most of them knew what was meant by:

> faint afternoons of Cups and Stakes and Handicaps.

None of them could get much further, even the girls who eventually passed English 'O' level. But this particular "slow learner" was the first to see that whilst race meetings came into the poem, they were not the heart of it. The key passage was about the horses' memories of their races, or whether, indeed, they had any:

> Do memories plague their ears like flies?
> They shake their heads.

In Michael's case it was possible to hint that if he had solved one problem so cleverly he could solve more, that his comprehension was coming on and that it would be worthwhile putting that much extra effort into his English. Ironically, a week before the exam, Michael broke his writing arm. The C.S.E. board allowed him to dictate his answers. The "essay" he produced was seven pages long and he gave good answers to the comprehension passages. And though we had predicted a borderline pass, the Board allowed him a Grade Three. One could argue that the amanuensis had produced correctly spelt and punctuated work. Yet when Michael left school, he was looking for a job on a farm. Few of his employers wanted to know how good his reading was let alone his writing : they would judge him on how competent he sounded.

In that C.S.E. exam no allowance was made for oral skills. In most of his lessons in Secondary School, talking out openly in class was penalised. The teachers' priorities had been whether pupils listened to what they said, then writing and then reading. Helping pupils, many of whom already have difficulties in speaking, to practise that very skill is often criticised as a nebulous, wishy-washy business, difficult to organize, impossible to assess and liable to lead to disciplinary problems.

For many of those teachers who are successful in getting Special Needs classes to learn through discussion, there seems to be a paradox at the heart of their work. They appear to want to anticipate as much of what will happen in their lesson as they can : yet they are also prepared to let the children have their say, get their own ideas straight and talk about them in their own way. Part of this anticipation may involve careful preparation for the lesson. The teacher works out his teaching objectives, then plans the kind of questions he will ask, and the kinds of replies he expects the children to make. Part of this preparation will be thinking out the dynamics of the group (Bion : 1961) which children are good at setting a discussion going, who needs time to work out an answer, who will need to be prompted. And part is the anticipation of problems. Some children will be likely to lose concentration, others will want to interrupt, and others will drift off into a private conversation.

Yet, despite all this careful planning and group assessment, those discussions from which children seem to learn most contain an element of unpredictability. They require teachers and pupils to improvise. In a discussion on Kes with low ability Fifth Years, we were trying to analyse the stylistic qualities the novel possessed. We had already written most of an essay, examining the plot and character: now we had to say what it was about the work as a whole that we liked. I had worked out that the class would probably talk about the realism and humour of the novel. We had looked the terms up in the dictionary in a previous lesson. And I thought that they would also want to pick out a favourite scene and work back from there. My ideas were summarised on the board, before the lesson began.

Derek the weakest reader in the class was expected to lead off because he was very quick with words, even though his concentration was limited. I thought Mark and Sidney would follow and I felt sure one of the more reflective girls like Sarah would follow up. I told the class this was a difficult thing to do and I wanted their fullest concentration, and having recapitulated what I was looking for, I asked Derek to start:

Teacher: Now Derek, you are good with words. What was there about this film you thought was really good?

Derek: Well I thought it was the language. It was the words people spoke, the way they spoke.

Teacher: Great Derek. Marvellous. What do you mean?

Derek: Well it was Yorkshire, wasn't it? People talking in a Yorkshire accent. It was good.

Teacher: Well thats great. I wasn't expecting that. Well done, Derek. Anybody else got any ideas about what was there in this film you thought was good?
(A few hands up including Mark's but not Sidney's or any of the girls').

What do you think Mark?

Mark: Well it was true to life, like.

Teacher: Yes great, what do you mean true to life, Mark?

Mark: Well it was like what happens to people. People in families. They are just like that. These things happen. It's just like in the book.

Teacher: Great. It's just like real life. Well done, Mark.
(There are still a few hands up, including rather a quiet boy called Chris who very rarely volunteers)

What's your idea, Chris?

Chris: It starts with disaster, then goes into triumph, then back down to disaster.

Teacher: Fantastic. I had not thought anyone would say that. What do you mean "disaster"?

Chris: Well not really disaster. At the beginning, his brother, well he picks on him. Then it's getting the bird. Then at the end it's disaster.

Some seven or eight of the pupils spoke in this way, working out their own ideas, reflecting on the shape and tone of the book with little prompting, until at last I asked Sarah what she thought. Normally highly imaginative and involved, all she could say was "It's boring."

After Sarah had finished, I reminded the class that they had to write a concluding paragraph to their "Kes" essays summarising the qualities the film and novel possessed. Those who had taken an active role in the discussion tackled this difficult task with considerable energy and insight. Derek wrote 250 words just on this section. Normally he was much more competent orally than with the written word. He tended to rush his work, making all kinds of spelling and grammatical errors and taking a superficial approach. Now he was much more careful with both presentation and ideas, as this extract shows:

> I have seen the video plus I have read the novel. I liked it very much becouse it is so realistic. The language is just right The Author is not to scard to use word. it show's how boring life can turn into exciting life but then back to boring life again
>
> The only work is down the pit but Now it is harder becouse of the strike. many people are out of work and many will be out of work for good. The best part of the video and book was when Billy trained the hawk in the video it showed it real good
>
> I realy liked reading and watching The book Kes. Its real good becouse it shows real life in a home in a mining town I though that The video was brillent. All the acter's were very good And they used the right expression to There parts. I did not like it much when Billy fround that his hawk was dead
>
> He did not use the right expression he just burried his head in the pillow and cried But then it got better when Billy started swinging his hawk around at Judd But Judd was just pushing him Away But then Billy started calling him names
>
> I think that Barry Hines has written a very good story which sum's up life in a mining town I have read most of his story's but This one is The one I like the most.

Despite the spelling mistakes, the misuse of apostrophes and capital letters and the difficulty Derek has in putting his thoughts into a logical order, one is aware of a mind grappling with the problems of literacy criticism. Many teachers would assume that for a child with his low reading age, (10.3) poor concentration and behavioural problems this would be quite impossible. But by helping Derek first explore his own ideas in discussion, with the teacher and the rest of the class as audience, he was encouraged to feel that he could do the same thing in writing. The depth of interest and understanding in Derek's conclusion can be compared to Sarah's. Sarah's reading is of a much higher standard than Derek's, her writing more competent and fluent, and she would probably get a higher mark in the exam for her essay than Derek. But without this active involvement in the class discussion, one feels she has learned so much less than him:

> I thought that the book couled Kes was not very good at all but the video was quite exciting. Some parts of the film was very sad especially where Judd, Billy's older brother had killed Kes. Billy was very upset and he wasn't able to hit Judd and his mother didn't lift a finger to help him. at all.

This is an honest response. She has caught the bleakness of the novel. And in terms of organization of ideas, this is a more competent conclusion. But Sarah makes her criticisms without substantiating them; whereas Derek shows how the very strength of the novel - its command of Northern working class dialect - makes us feel let down at the crucial moment when Billy learns of the hawk's death. I had not told the class either that the language was what made the novel or that there was moments where one felt that Hines' writing had been weak. The first point arose directly out of what the pupils said, the second came as Derek was writing. The reason he had been able to think it out was, one suspects, because the class had taken his original idea seriously in the discussion.

Getting pupils actively involved in speaking and listening involves more than thorough preparation and an awareness of the speaking styles of the children in one's class, however. It is at least as important to learn something of the language children use. Older pupils in Special Needs groups often adopt the broadest variations of the local dialect and if the starting teacher has never met West Indian Creole Speakers or Geordies, he is likely to find such pupils unintelligible.

This is a difficult and controversial area and simple staffroom observation will reveal a considerable range of opinion amongst teachers. At one extreme there are those who discount all dialect words as slang and dialect formations as ungrammatical. As far as is within their power, they would exclude the local speech from their classroom. They would argue that because of their accents, children fail to sound out their words "properly" and this affects their spelling.

There are others, who following the theories of Basil Bernstein (1971), would argue that working class speech uses a "restricted code", which limit the linguistic and conceptual complexity of speech and so inhibits educational progress. According to Bernstein's research, working class adolescents use fewer nouns, more pronouns and fewer relative clauses than their middle class peers. He thought that this restricted the range of topics open for discussion, inhibited the interplay of abstract ideas and tied meaning to "local relationships and local social structures".

Theories of linguistic deprivation like Bernstein's were immediately attacked. Another sociolinguist who has heavily influenced teachers' thinking is Labov (1969). He argued that the absence of particles, the dropping of the letter 's' from the ends of verbs, the use of 'me' instead of 'I' and "them" instead of "they" are quite consistent within a given dialect. In terms of West Indian Ceole or Negro Non-Standard English they can be traced back to underlying West African syntactical patterns. Labov claims that, faced with linguistic researchers using standard English, the non-standard users become confused and inarticulate. But researchers who are capable of developing rapport with them and demonstrating interest in the non-standard forms find that these speech patterns are as capable of generating complex thought as Standard English. Other researchers have argued that whilst there are slight differences in speech patterns between working class and middle class children before they come to school, it is the experience of schools which exacerbates these differences and makes them so important for educational attainments (Wells)

Whatever the strengths of these sociolinguistic theories, it could be argued that more time should be allowed those who are starting to teach children with special needs to observe classroom discussions and experiment with a wide range of discussion techniques and situations.

Working with backward readers in the Special Needs Department can provide a starting point. One breaks up the reading with discussions about the book, what will happen next and so on. The lesson can finish with a few minutes informal chat about the children's interests and what has been happening to them. It may be possible to take small groups out of Special Schools or Special Classes on educational visits and so spend part of the day talking informally with them. Helping with School Sports Teams or on a practical task may help too.

As part of their work experience programmes for pupils with Special Needs, many schools get groups decorating parts of their own buildings. These can provide ideal situations in which to observe pupil talk and group processes, and so, one hopes, find ways of overcoming barriers to communication. A few schools have off site buildings which are periodically redecorated by groups of "non-exam" pupils.

On the last evening of one such expedition, we had a discussion about how these pupils felt about time out of school and how they were looking forward to the world of work. The group knew each other very well, but I was a relative stranger. So it took some time for them to come together and find a way of talking to me.

One of the group, Billy, was a long term truant. He had been diagnosed by his G.P. as depressed and he had been receiving treatment from a child psychiatrist. He hardly ever went out and had several times threatened his mother when she had tried to force him to go to school. In the discussion, he was very nervous of my tape recorder and though capable of being lucid and thoughtful on a one-to-one basis, he found the formal discussion quite overwhelming. It was as relaxed as I could make it, we had just had a huge meal and we were sitting round a log fire with cups of coffee in our hands. But trying to articulate his feelings about the week to this small group and an adult led to a few jumbled phrases like the adolescents Labov describes, Billy's speech eventually collapses into silence:

Teacher: Can you remember about any meals you've been doing and how you feel about coming away?

Billy: Been cooking ... er .. I'll tell .. er .. on t' barbeque .. then we brought it back in .. Making rice pudding with ...

Mel had been sent to a Special School and had just returned so that he could leave school from a Comprehensive and thus avoid the social stigma of a Special School reference for an employer. His reading and writing had been very poor and his behaviour difficult. His position in the group was almost as insecure as Billy's and he felt torn between his desire for acceptance by his peers and his need to appear "reformed" to staff. When asked what he enjoyed most, he was similarly hesitant and confused:

Teacher: What was the thing you enjoyed most about this week?

Mel: Walking.

Teacher: Tell us which walk you enjoyed most.

Mel: .. The hill walk .. last night ...

Teacher: Go on ...

Mel: .. Can't think of nowt ..

Even with the boys who felt quite happy with the group and relaxed about joining in a discussion, there was an unsureness about what the teacher wanted. What were they supposed to say? Should they give the teacher what he wanted to hear, or rebel against his authority and "have a laugh"? What did the rest of the group feel and how could they find out without the risk of "showing themselves up"? when asked what he had got most out of, Jim replied so softly that the microphone hardly picked it up: "Workin'":

Teacher: Tell us about the work you've been doing.

Jim: Been stripping walls and .. er .. filling holes in (it) which were left over and painting.

Teacher: Tell us about why you enjoyed it.

Jim: I don't know. It's just getting rid on t' school.

Teacher: Right. Tell us how that's felt, getting rid of school?

Jim: Brilliant .. I don't like school.

Teacher: Why?

Jim: 'Cos it's boring.

Teacher: What's so different about the work you've been doing this week?

Jim: 'Cos it's useful.

Jim found it difficult it express such negative feelings himself and though his voice got louder with the phrase "getting rid out' school", one still sensed his reluctance to talk, his inability to resolve the tensions within the group. However, once he had started and once the teacher had shown he wanted people to be honest about their feelings, however negative, others in the group could talk with greater fluency and clarity. Jim had created a register for the group (Barnes : 1969) without actually being able to take advantage of it himself. If anything David and Chris were less intelligent and had lower attainments than the other two but by the time they spoke the dynamics of the group had shifted. They knew now how the others all felt and that they could speak for them. They felt enabled to trust the teacher and ignore the tape recorder:

Teacher: Does anyone want to add anything to what Jim's just said?

David: I do .. ha ... I've learnt more here than I have at school. Learned how to paint .. and er ..

Teacher: Don't you learn that at school?

David: No I don't do Art or owt like that at school. I do woodwork and things like that .. er .. I enjoyed walk an' all, one that we done today, comin' down t' moors when you dropped us off at t' top. It were great .. it were good. You could run like 'ell down it.

Teacher: Right, pass the tape over to Chris.

Chris: Best thing is we're out of school. We've learned a lot more here than we are (sic) at school. Don't get French or owt like that. Get a good reference when you leave school. Get more chance of a job if you get a good reference. It gives us time

> out. A bit of an 'oliday as well, when you've done your work.

Even this short extract from the beginning of the discussion shows how as trust deepens within a group, individual talkers become more settled, more reflective and able to use fuller, more complex sentences. Billy and Mel seem to grab at ideas and images and to be unable to fuse them into coherent statements. Earlier in the week Billy had helped make a barbeque, tried cooking some sausages on it, realised they would take too long, brought them into the kitchen and finished them off under a grill. He knew that I knew what had happened and it seems pointless telling me what I already knew. On the other hand he is unsure about how a description of his feelings will be received by the rest of the group. So he collapses into silence. However, once Jim had begun to test how much the teacher would tolerate by expressing some of the group's negative feeling about school, the others were freed to explore their experiences. The way that Jim asserted "rid" ("getting <u>rid</u> on t' school") signalled a rush of energy, a depth of feeling and a preparedness to be honest almongst them all. When he said that, no one, not even the teacher, could be sure which way the conversation would go, and it was this small degree of uncertainty which gave the last two speakers their sense of vitality and confidence.

There are syntactical errors even in Chris' speech: "We've learned a lot more than we are at school." There are also clearly distinguishable instances of Yorkshire dialect, which could well appear ungrammatical to the 'O' level English language examiner, but which are part of a consistent and comprehensible speech pattern: "comin' down t' moors .. it were good." Chris' speech repudiates many of the points Bernstein makes about the minutiae of adolescent working class speech. He elides the nominative pronoun and uses two "logical operators" in three sentences:

> Don't get French or owt like that. Get a good reference <u>when</u> you leave school. Get more chance of a job <u>if</u> you get a good reference"

Localised group expectations are of great importance in the way these ideas about the usefulness of their work developed. Yet they helped rather than hindered the use of the "reflective" mode which

Bernstein marks out as such an important characteristic of elaborated middle class speech patterns. Where Billy and Mel found the discussion very difficult, David and Chris are able to make use of their friends' ideas and feelings in order to reflect on the experience and then express their own views. Billy's grammar collapsed under the strain and his ideas were inexplicable to anyone who had not been there. Whilst Chris' speech patterns were non-standard they were clear and consistent and one felt he was not only thinking, he was expressing his thoughts simply and concisely. The most significant difference between these two speakers was not their individual speech skills. On a one-to-one basis Billy had often demonstrated during that week how articulate he could be. What was important was the linguistic context within which they spoke. When Billy started the discussion, the group was unsure what could be said and in what manner. By the time Chris spoke, there was a sense of confidence in what they felt and how it would be received. A sense of a receptive audience had been created.

How quickly one develops that receptivity depends to a certain extent on the group's previous experience of discussion work. There are a number of techniques teachers have developed to speed that process. Some have adapted the idea of a conch shell from "The Lord of the Flies" (Golding) and in order to get the group to listen to a designated speaker, they have a symbolic mace to pass around. Others use word games, like making up stories by adding a word each in turn. Others start with small scale drama exercises between pairs. The children are asked to explain the lesson topic to each other as if they are on the telephone. And for teachers working in Science or Practical subjects, parts of a message are given to different members of a group. The group has then to assemble the message through group discussion and carry out the instructions before all the other groups have done. (Dolan : et al)

In some schools these very small scale oral activities are almost unnecessary. The children appreciate the need not to shout out all at once, but to listen to what each member of the class has to say. In one first year Maths class for slow learners, the teacher had divided the children into groups of twos and threes and then set them some long division problems to solve. These involved a fair amount of estimation.

The more organized the groups were in apportioning and reporting back their guesses, the quicker the problems were solved. The class went to work very excitedly and competition was intense. When eventually this part of the lesson came to an end and the class had to listen to the teacher, they fell silent immediately. They enjoyed the small group discussions immensely and wanted more of them. But they could also distinguish quite clearly between a part of a lesson where they were encouraged to talk and listen to one another, and a part where they just had to listen quietly. This degree of receptiveness made one feel they could easily cope with whole group discussions. At the end of the lesson, one of these Special Needs pupils even said, "Ooh Sir, long division is so interesting !"

Among Special Needs groups in general, however, such immediate understanding is quite a rarity. Many pupils have had little experience of discussion work. Some divide what happens in school into two categories: work (which means writing) and messing about. For a teacher to tell them that at one moment they must solve a problem through discussion and at another they must fall silent and listen to him can create a lot of confusion. The small group activities raise the emotional temperature in the classroom. The more dominant children won't solve all the problems. Children who find it difficult to put their ideas into words can get very frustrated. Even if the teacher has given the class a very definite time limit, there are those who find the task so strange and off putting, they revert to safer topics of conversation, what was on the television last night or who is going out with whom. Even on topics about which the teacher would expect high pupil motivation, it takes time for the groups to create that sense of audience we noted in the previous extract. So when one is starting to use discussion work with Special Needs groups, it is extremely important to explain what one is doing before and after the discussion, to praise pupils who spoke and listened well and to tell the class what one does not want.

These comments and explanations have the effect of putting a "frame" round the experience. If a class is used to thinking of discussion lessons as "mucking about" even three minutes problem solving can generate a lot of restlessness. Once launched into a conversation, several of the class will need to be reminded about the need to be quiet again. Those who took little part in small group discussion will need to be actively involved in the lesson again. Those who have got involved in arguments will need to be given time to "cool off". The clearer one makes one's comments and the more one gets a class to appreciate that talking can be a serious and demanding intellectual activity, the less they are likely to regard discussion lessons as an opportunity to test out the teacher.

With some Special Needs groups, it may be quite some time before the teacher is confident enough to start full scale whole-class discussions. For me in my first teaching post in an Inner-City Comprehensive it was half term before I began them with Special Needs classes. Even that was after I had spent several lessons observing other staff with similar classes to mine and after I had seen another teacher using discussion techniques with my group. The advantage of trying small group work and games will be that one already knows which children are likely to dominate whole class discussions, who easily gets bored and so on. Part of the "framing" of these large scale discussions will involve telling certain children that one wants them to start, that one wants others to limit themselves to three or four points, that one will be very cross if another one does not listen, and that one would be very pleased if these other children told the group what they thought. With many more children to wait their turn it becomes all the harder for them to hold their ideas in their minds. By the time that it is their turn to speak, the conversation may well have moved on from their original point, and yet many of these children will find it difficult to update their ideas. Such problems will add to the group's frustrations, but it is all the more important to emphasise before, during and after discussions that their ultimate aim is to create a situation where all listen to each. No matter what the temptation, no-one may interrupt another.

However carefully one plans and frames the whole group discussion, it is quite likely that the most effective learning comes from that element of unpredictability, when members of the group bring in feelings that have not been accepted before or ideas they did not know they had. Taking advantage of these moments requires considerable personal skill and confidence from the teacher. If one is having a discussion about something which the pupils feel very strongly, arguments become not only heated but personal. Even experienced teachers can feel overwhelmed and uncertain. In the middle of one whole class discussion I was recently having with a group of eighteen bottom stream school leavers on "Society and Animals", the class very rapidly split into the majority who thought fox hunting was a cruel and most despicable activity and an equally passionate minority who enjoyed participating in it. In the heat of the moment, one of this minority suddenly went very red and his eyes filled with tears. He stood up and for a moment I was unsure whether he would hit one of his tormentors or run out of the room. One could not say, "Come on Michael, it's only a discussion" because this particular child always found it difficult to distinguish between rational debate and personal invective. One had to change the subject very quickly and silence any members of the group tempted to goad him further.

Assessing the temperature of a discussion, keeping a stock of questions ready to change the subject, either to involve more children or to cool somebody off, encouraging a breadth of vision and yet minimising irrelevancies requires considerable dexterity from someone starting to teach Special Needs groups. And having said all that, there are still discussions with even the most able and experienced teachers which go wrong. The children seem to be talking all at once and about anything but the topic of the lesson, little thought is put into the speeches and the class appears restless and demoralised. The teacher's voice is now one amongst many and it is easy to feel threatened. Toni, a student on teaching practice in the slow learners' hut in a depressed Northern steel town said she felt at her most helpless at moments like this. She felt that the pupils had seen through her role playing. She had been found out, exposed and the audience had taken over the playhouse. The logic of the situation demanded that she reassert herself and she longed to storm at the children, restoring her own sense of self esteem by humiliating them.

However, as this student pointed out, shouting at a class in a discussion lesson is at best only a temporary measure. The class go quiet for a while, then the noise rises again. The children are now much more restless and less willing to listen to each other or the teacher. The only way out is to reassert oneself firmly but calmly. The student described how she had learned this lesson for herself. The slow learners' hut was isolated from the rest of the school, at the far end of the playground. It was a very windy day and the children all seemed highly strung. Some wild dogs had come on to the playground and chased them during breaktime. Toni had not realised what had happened, but the class had been extremely restless and the discussion with which she had planned to open the lesson collapsed. After trying to force them to listen to each other, she had taken the decision to abandon her lesson. She took out her guitar and sang to them. Gradually this calmed the group down and she finished the lesson with some written exercises and drawing. As the bell went for the end of the period, she told them that when she took them again next day, they would have their discussion and the creative writing she had planned for them. She did exactly that and produced some very good work. She had presented a calm exterior and acted in a determined way. Had she not done so she said she thought it would have been difficult to get the class to take her or her discussion lesson seriously, again.

Whilst it is rare to have Special Needs groups as receptive as the "Long Division" group described above, it is almost equally as rare to find them in states of such high excitement as Toni's. For many students oral work with the bottom set or "remedial" classes can be one of the most satisfying aspects of a teaching practice. Suzanne, another student started by telling the class stories and getting them to tell them back to her. She read plays with them, then got them to perform them, then improvise their own. It was a regular thing at the end of the week for them to read their work to the class and have an informal discussion about their hobbies and interests. Some children were more restless than others, some spoke too much, some were too argumentative or bitchy, others always wanted to start private conversations with their friends rather then address the group as a whole. But with a sharp look here, a warning there, the class could be coaxed into listening to one another, creating an audience for themselves.

By praising a class when it begins to work in a way which the teacher feels happy with, and by giving them the experience of being listened to and appreciated, the class can be educated into seeing talk and active listening as important aspects of learning, into seeing themselves as a group who can work and talk together. Many of the teachers who regularly use discussion with Special Needs groups find that though there is a place for silence, pupils often work better when allowed to talk. And it is at the stage when talk is an accompaniment to work, as a way of exploring ideas and re-asserting the integrity of a group that the kind of ethos one noted in that Liverpool E.S.N. [Subnormal] (M) school begins to emerge. Despite all the difficulties and anxieties it brings, this use of pupil talk and pupil listening can produce work of a very high standard and can render the class receptive to the most subtle of teacher controls.

REFERENCES

Barnes, D. (1969) Language in the Secondary Classroom: in Language, the Learner and the School Ed Barnes, D. et al. Penguin

Bion, W.R. (1961) Experience in Groups : Tavistock Publications

Bernstein, B. (1971) Class Codes and Control : Routledge and Kegan Paul

Dolan, T. et al (1979) Improving Reading Through Group Discussion Activities in The Effective Use of Reading : Ed Lunzer, E. and Gardner, K. Heinemann

Golding, W. (1978) Lord of the Flies : Coward

Hines, B. (1976) A Kestrel for a Knave : Heinemann

Labov, W. (1979) The Logic of Non Standard English: in Language and Social Context : Ed Giglioni, P.P. Penguin

Larkin, P. At Grass

Wells, G. (1981) Learning Through Interaction: C.U.P.

Chapter Four

WRITING AND EXAMINATIONS

After a few days' observation in a local Comprehensive, one of our mature students with teaching experience abroad reported back to her College seminar group that she did not like what she had seen of the Special Needs Department. There had been very little reading or discussion. Instead, the pupils had had to spend lesson after lesson on written work. This might not have been so bad if only the writing tasks had been constructive. But so many of the lessons involved copying from books or from the blackboard. They were given exercises requiring simple - often mechanical - answers. In English, they had to do "grammar work" and when she looked at their notebooks, they were filled with spelling tests and comprehensions. Of course, she recognised that children with faulty syntax and poor spelling needed help, but this work seemed to have been given out to the class as a whole, irrespective of individuals' needs. She thought it was scarcely surprising that so many of the pupils had "learning difficulties" even after they had left school. They had never been given a chance to produce anything that meant something to them. There was no meaning in their work. Writing, she concluded, was a cynical exercise designed to keep the children occupied.

Others in the seminar thought that the picture she had drawn was much too harsh. One of them disagreed, though. Gerry argued that such an approach to teaching children with Special Needs merely reflected the priorities of the Secondary School system as a whole. All the other children in the school were expected to produce some writing in every lesson, too, and for many of them these written tasks were mechanical and irrelevant. While for the great majority all this writing practice led to an exam pass, it could only deepen the sense of futility felt by those with learning difficulties. In most subjects, exam passes were restricted to the top 80% of the ability range. Gerry thought it must be clear to teachers and pupils alike that the vast majority of children with Special Needs were expected to fail. He argued that for any widespread change in special provision, the examination system would have to be recast.

For some of those involved in Special Education, it is being recognised that the exam system indirectly affects the learning attainments of the children traditionally excluded from it. The sense that they have no qualifications to work for itself affectsthe motivation of "non-exam" classes.

If children with Special Needs could be given something definite to aim at, if they were judged in such a way that their positive qualities were reinforced and if schooling led to a recognised assessment, the standard of their written work might rise. It has been argued, notably by Sir Keith Joseph, that if the format of the exam system were changed, so that they were used to measure children's attainments against "objective" criteria, it might be possible to raise the standards of the least able 40%. At present exam passes are "norm-referenced"; that is to say the grade one gets depends on where one is placed on the overall ability distribution. Originally a child in the middle of the ability range received a Grade 4 C.S.E. If the exams were criteria-referenced, so the children were measured against well defined skill-levels, some have suggested that this bottom 40% could even get C.S.E. Grade 4.

Most teachers have reacted sceptically. A key phrase for Special Needs staff is, "You don't fatten pigs by weighing them". There is no research evidence to back up these claims. Yet, if one has a close look at some of the criteria of exams already in use, it seems a little surprising that after eleven years of schooling, even those with learning difficulties could not achieve success. These criteria are freely available from the exam boards themselves. A Grade 6 C.S.E. - or fail grade - in the Yorkshire and Humberside Regional Board means that:

> At this level, the candidate cannot communicate clearly. His written English is so weak it obscures his meaning.

On one of the essays presented for the 1984 Agreement Trials, there is a further comment. Whilst there are "coherent sections" in a Grade 6 piece, "sentence structure breaks down" and "the essay becomes increasingly confused". This lack of coherence is undoubtedly a crucial problem for pupils with a history of reading difficulties. One wonders, however, whether this is solely due to underlying intellectual and linguistic problems in the child or whether the school context has its part to play, too. It is not merely College Students who have noticed how much time a Special Needs Department give to the technical minutiae of written work - spelling, punctuation and comprehension. The Bullock Committee pointed out the over-dependence on grammar exercises, project work and other forms of copying. (H.M.S.O. 1975). Viv Furlong (1977), Rachel Sharp and Antony Green (1975) have commented that teachers and less able pupils view such "busywork" with complacency. Resentful older pupils might view someone as a "good teacher" because a class writes a lot of pages in their notebooks each lesson. The fact that none of the pupils' ideas went into the work is not as important as the quantity of work done or the feeling that something has been produced.

Against such a set of pupil expectations, it is clear that to expect pupils to generate their own ideas in coherent prose will require considerable preparation. Just as some pupils have to be educated into talking and listening to each other, so they have to learn how to assemble sequences of ideas, so as to create a meaningful whole. If they have never done this before, it can be quite a threatening experience. The work of the following pupil, Karen, gives an example of the problems of those who have started the reading process but who have not yet learned how to put across what they want to in writing.

Karen was part of a class which had had to do a lot of written exercises. As part of this particular lesson, they were told the Dracula story. They had all listened intently and with apparent comprehension. After the teacher had told the story, they had sat around a tape recorder telling bits of the story in turn. Some had grasped the main ideas well enough to interject material of their own. The pupils' tape had then been played back to them so that in all they had heard the story three times. They were then told to write it up. This is Karen's version, with spelling and punctuation corrected:

> Dracula
>
> It started in London. He was named by Jonathon. Jonathan went to Count von Transylvania. He got a lift from Count von Transylvania to the castle.
>
> He got a private letter. He opened it up and it said, "Count von Transylvania. Come to the castle because I want to buy some of your houses".
>
> The man said, "You will have to pay sixty pounds. Will that do?" "Yes,"said Jonathan.
>
> He got fed pork, beef, potatoes, cakes and red wine and white wine and Jonathan said to Doctor van Helsing.

What Karen had done was to pick out details of the story and put them together in a jumbled sequence. The result for most readers is that meaning is lost. What she had been trying to suggest was that Jonathan had received the letter from the Count asking him to come to his castle so that the Count could buy some houses from him. When he had got near the castle, the villagers had been so frightened they refused to take him there for less than sixty pounds. The villagers abandoned him some way from the castle, so the Count himself had had to give him a lift in his carriage. After a huge supper that night, Jonathan discovered the evils of Castle Dracula. He had then escaped but with the help of Doctor van Helsing he had eventually defeated Count Dracula.

Karen had a lot of difficulty starting her story. She sat and thought about it a long time. What she had done, though, was to set the scene and describe the hero as if she were answering a Comprehension exercise, "It started in London. He was named by Jonathan." She states the facts baldly, as if they have objective value beyond the conventions of this story. She moves from one part of the story to another without seemingly understanding the narrative sequence. She does not seem able to place the village carriage driver or Doctor van Helsing.

The clearest evidence that Karen has no clear grasp of this task comes in the penultimate paragraph. The list of food could again be the answer to a comprehension question about what did Jonathan eat. The major point of this description had been a dramatic irony, which had not escaped the class. While Jonathan eats, the Count watches. When Jonathan invites the Count to join him, he replies "I will eat no animal's flesh." When Jonathan offers him red wine, the Count says "I will not drink the juice of the grape." The class understood that the Count prefers human flesh and blood and that whilst they knew that the Count van Transylvania was Dracula, Jonathan did not.

Students of English Literature would point out that dramatic ironies like this convey part of the structure of the narrative They do not just embellish the story, but are important to our understanding of the whole. One could argue that in certain sections Karen does have some sort of "feel" for the story, but that she has other expectations of story lessons which keep making her "lose the thread". The rapport there had been between herself and the story teller, had been almost lost by the time Karen had put pen to paper.

Many linguists would argue that an understanding of narrative is a prerequisite to the handling of sequences of ideas in other modes. It is highly likely that a child who finds difficulty with Dracula will also have problems with relating cause and effect in Science or History or understanding processes in other subject areas. Karen may well have been able to "take notes" on these processes, when this meant copying from textbook or blackboard. She could also have "done a worksheet". But one wonders what this would have meant to her. Faced with the question, "Do you understand what you have to write, Karen?" She might have thought the teacher really meant, "Do you remember sufficient facts to keep you busy for the duration of the writing lesson?"

A constant diet of copying worksheets and projects can almost innoculate children against their inner sense of the meaning of a lesson, and teachers across the curriculum may have to think of strategies to overcome this. One of my students started teaching practice by constantly asking his classes, "Have you got that?" Not only did it break the flow of the lesson and irritate the children, the simple Yes/No answer he was looking for was of little help to him in determining what they had made of his teaching. He then had to build up the kind of talking and listening skills which enabled the pupils to discuss with him what they thought he had been teaching them.

It is fatally easy to assume that a group of

children with learning difficulties has understood the main points of a lesson, just because they can answer questions on it.

A lesson on the Geography of the Nile had started with a vivid description of the way Egypt stands from year to year in the baking heat, with hardly a drop of rain. Mysteriously once a year the River Nile rises and floods the fields next to it. This allows crops to grow and so has enabled the Egyptians to have one of the oldest civilizations in the world. The slow learners group had a Geography textbook, with the right readability level. This explained how the rain fell in the Mountains to the South once a year. There were photographs of the Nile in flood and at its lowest point, photographs of the Mountains, the Egyptian desert, the riverside fields and the Delta. Before the lesson had begun a cartoon was drawn on the blackboard showing the Mountains where the Nile rises, the long journey through the desert and the Delta where it passed into the sea. Storm clouds gathered over the mountains, rain fell and the Nile acted like a drain carrying off the excess water.

Using these three modes - oral description, text books with reading material and photographs and blackboard cartoon, one felt sure they would understand the sequence of ideas, so the class was asked, "Do you understand?" They snorted that of course they did. One of them was then picked to explain the way that the Nile floods. None of them could. So we went through the explanation again. This time the class admitted they were still not sure, but one or two volunteered some ideas. They saw that the Nile had three main sections, that it only rained heavily in the Mountains and that this happened once a year. But even now they failed to grasp that the large amount of water that fell in the mountains transmitted itself to an area where normally next to no rain fell. The basic paradox with which the lesson had started, that water suddenly arrived in the desert once a year and made life possible eluded them. This was the key to all our subsequent lessons - Ancient Egyptian agriculture, the modern damming policy and to most of the factual information about population and economic development in our Geography textbooks. Eventually after one explained again how mysterious the rising of the river must have appeared to the Egyptians some of the class began to appreciate the sequence of ideas for themselves. It was now their turn to pass on their ideas to the rest of the class.

By the end of the lesson, we had drawn and labelled cartoons and made a summary of the process which caused the Nile to rise and the effects it had on the land. The children wrote between 50 and 200 words outlining these processes, a considerable achievement for many of them, but little in comparison to the intellectual effort involved in explaining the pattern to the teacher and their peers. Without this discussion, I would not have realized where the lesson had gone wrong and only a few of the class would have seen the point of it.

Faced with a class of children with learning difficulties many teachers ask themselves two questions, "How can I make my class quiet long enough to teach them something?" and "How can I then occupy them so they will then carry on quietly?" They then conduct a lesson which places few intellectual demands on the children and give them exercises and drawings to do to follow this up. The teacher may not expect the children to understand or remember much of the lesson, anyway, so poor marks in an end of term test is seen as the pupils' fault. Getting the pupils to tell him what they did or did not understand requires a different form of control. In order to get the pupils to succeed, the teacher has to be prepared to admit that he himself will often fail to communicate his ideas. Enabling pupils with learning difficulties to write about their lessons in coherent prose is a much more thorough test of one's teaching than keeping them quiet, or getting them to answer questions. Yet a lesson where one has allowed the pupils to explain your ideas to each other and then written them down in their own words, one finds they understand and retain much more. It is after such lessons, when the pupils' writing is read out to the class and some are asked to copy theirs out for display on the walls that one begins to convince some of them that they can indeed write well.

James is perhaps an extreme example of a child whose belief in himself as a writer was a prime factor in learning to write. His parents had always known that he was not as slow as his school attainments made him out to be. In many ways he appeared to be the typically "dull" child. He thought slowly, he lost concentration very easily, he was slow to catch on to new ideas, he even spoke in a dull and monotonous way. His primary teachers could never decide whether he had general learning difficulties or particular problems in reading. A psychologist who tested him said that whilst his attainments were in the subnormal range, his IQ was a little higher.

When he arrived at the comprehensive school, he was an undersized, immature, bewildered boy who could barely copy from the blackboard. He day dreamed a lot and this had disastrous effects in many areas of the curriculum. In Maths, for instance, he could lose the thread whilst working on sums like "What is two less than eight?" The writing breakthrough came after the Christmas break. During the holidays the film "E.T." had been shown and this had thoroughly captivated James. He had a battery operated model of E.T., whose finger he could light up. He constantly played with this for a week and had it on top of or underneath the desk in lessons, depending on which teacher was taking him. One day he asked if he could be excused the story that the others had been asked to write and do his own E.T. story. Having set the others off the teacher got James to say what he wanted to write, showed him how to split it into three chapters, the beginning, the adventures of James and E.T. and the departure and put some spellings on the blackboard. Even with all this help, James would not start at once. He wanted to make the story his own, he had to structure it in his own way. This meant going into a dream, staring round the room for several minutes:

"What are you doing, James?"

"I'm thinking, Sir"

Eventually he started his laborious printing, but every five or six lines he had to stop for more "thinking". He was still writing when everybody else in the group had finished, and he carried on after the bell had gone.

His story was set in the village where he lived. He was walking home one night after school when he heard E.T. scuffling and crying in the hedgerow. Using simple monosyllabic words, James made the reader feel he was there. Whereas in the film, it was the technological splendour of E.T.'s craft and the impersonal hostility of the adults that first catch our attention, James had realized that with or without the space craft, the meeting between E.T. and a boy like himself would be just as momentous.

James invites E.T. home with him and in the

morning E.T. asks James to come away with him. He decides he cannot, a "triangle of lights" comes down on James' lawn, E.T. goes home and James returns to school. Even though James had rarely managed to write more than a few lines in his life before, he had now written two sides. Despite the constant stops for daydreams, he rarely seemed to lose his way. E.T. existed clearly in his mind's eye before he began the story, he already had a wealth of feelings and fantasies to draw on and he knew what was likely to happen. The writing process itself and the reflection which permeated it allowed him to work out exactly what happened and how it hung together.

As one might expect of a child with a reading age of seven, there were no full stops and the spelling was chaotic. When corrections were made and he had written out a fair copy, it was obvious to everyone that it was a very good story. The fair copy was mounted and displayed. It was read back to James' class and to other groups in the same year. Not only did quite a few write their own E.T. story it allowed others to grasp the value of a three part structure to their fiction : arrival, adventures and departure.

From now on James only needed to be reminded of this kind of structure in order to produce more of his own stories. The idea of paragraphing arose spontaneously from class discussions about how to arrange material. The three sections were redefined as three paragraphs. We looked at the books we had been reading to see what was meant by "indenting" the new paragraph. And in this way, James' work became the model for grammatical work with the rest of the class, with the teacher deducing the "rules" of paragraphing from what they had already learned in the process of writing. Later we brought in the punctuation of speech in a similar way. The pupils felt the need to put in speech. We showed how this could be used to heighten the effect of a story that one of them had written. Lastly we looked at the rules of punctuating speech.

James suffered the same kind of vertigo writers seem to experience after their first book is published. He felt he would never be able to repeat the success of that first story. It also gave him new responsibilities. Instead of being allowed to write a few lines and say, "Please, Miss, I can't write any more." he was now made to feel he had to produce stories with dilemmas, climaxes and unexpected endings, to attempt History essays and accounts of Scientific experiments, and to cover a page or more. In spite of this, his confidence grew. As it did, he learned that he did not have to "think" about the story, in pauses between the writing of it, but that he could think and write at the same time. These were not lessons that one could consciously teach a child with learning difficulties in the same way as one could teach speech marks or plurals or comprehension. The motivation had to come from within the pupil. James had to feel that he could deal with the problems of spelling this particular word and form those particular letters at the same time as forging the overall pattern of the story in his mind.

The problem for the teacher was how to keep the self confidence and sense of involvement alive, in spite of the immensity of these technical problems and in spite of the fact that his marks in the school's exams made him feel a failure, once again. He was given no credit for the advances he had made. He had come last in virtually every subject and he knew it. In the second year, James' reading began to improve very fast, thanks mainly to his enjoyment of the James Herriot vet books. Herriot actually worked in our town, and lived in the same village as two of the boys in James' class. Many of the people and places in his stories could still be identified. The publishers had adapted the easy reading version so that each story lasted a couple of lessons. The humour and local language were greatly appreciated.

We had not written letters before so we started with a letter to a real person - James Herriot. Again one forgets how difficult it can be to learn a skill like laying out a letter head. Some of the group mixed up the top right of the page with the top left. In some cases the pupils lived in a town with street names and numbers, whilst others had house names and villages. Trying to explain the order in which each one went was very difficult, especially as some had "done letters before" in Primary School and wanted to plunge into the letter immediately, whether or not they had got the letter head right. We had to have five different forms of address on the blackboard before all of them understood their own particular layout.

We then discussed what we were to write. Gradually the group settled and then James asked, "Can I be cheeky?" He had written about how one of his favourite bits was where Herriot had helped a hill farmer with a sow in labour. One of the piglets had got stuck and died inside the sow. Herriot had had to pull that out. By now the sow was too exhausted to push the rest out, so Herriot had to pull them out, too. As he put his had inside, one piglet had bitten his finger. Herriot had sworn, pulled it out and said, "Well at least that one's alive." James had finished his letter by asking the author to come into school to meet his teacher:

> He's not too bad and at least he doesn't bite.

This humorous touch was read out to the rest of the class, who immediately wanted to include something amusing of their own in their own letters. Fair copies were made and duly despatched to the author. He made a very courteous reply, which was then read out to the whole year in assembly. The children concerned were really excited for the rest of the day and it no doubt made them rather silly. But in the long term, it helped confirm their feeling that they were good writers, in spite of any exam marks. They could produce something that was sensible, worthwhile and original.

After the group had finished the Herriot books, they began another adaptation, this time of Shane. This led them to a task normally conceived of as far too demanding for children with a history of reading difficulties - literary criticism. In order to do this, we had to overturn many of the conventions in the schooling of children with learning difficulties. As well as asking them to examine problems of tone and structure, we had to ask them to say what they honestly liked and disliked. So often children with learning difficulties dismiss all school work, all reading and all writing as "boring". Even before they begin they expect their work will be a failure. It would be perverse to appear to be enjoying anything which gave so little pay-off, so they reject teachers, books and writing before they themselves are rejected. Real problems of relationship or literary appropriateness are drowned out in the general unwillingness to risk more failure.

"Shane" does present such problems. These become particularly obvious when classes are shown the film adaption starring Alan Ladd. Shane himself is constantly described as a "mysterious" man in Schaefer's book. For some reason we never fully understood, he has decided to give up gun fighting and the beginning of the story is deliberately slow and free of violent incident. Shane's aggression only becomes clear when he uproots an old tree stump and he even refuses the challenge of a raw cow-hand. It is only in the second half of both novel and film that he uses his fists and then his gun.

This book challenges a number of pupils' expectations. Many of the American films they see on T.V. show heroes who have no compunction about using the most extreme forms of violence. In series like "The A Team" there is little sense of dilemma and scenes of fist fights and armed violence are lengthy and frequent. The sound track of such films is often deliberately noisy and distracting, colours are vivid and action - explicit. Yet Shane's aggression is often only implied and Ladd's portrayal for the most part calm and underplayed. The female lead - Jean Arthur - is a homely, gentle lady, twice Ladd's age, loyal to her husband, vulnerable and deeply opposed to violence. No Farrah Fawcett Major or Wonder Woman.

James' group for the most part found the film "boring" and yet they understood the way the slow build up led to the climaxes of explosive violence. When they wrote essays about it, they could see the relevance of the tree stump incident to the eventual gunfight. They knew what Shane was like and they understood that these earlier unspectacular scenes helped make the eventual shoot out more exciting. An awareness of the interpendence of the structure and tone of the novel, was then transferred into their own stories making them much more sophisticated.

In a very few schools, where there has been a consistent policy of inter-relating reading, talking, listening and writing in the first three years, it is possible for children with a history of learning difficulties to be prepared for external examinations. Even in these schools, there are considerable doubts, not least among the pupils. After years of coming last in school based exams and feeling themselves to be failures, pupils have to be taught to see themselves as capable of success.

One way of boosting self concepts is to ensure that these pupils are seen to be involved in high status school activities and relate the writing to this. One half term theme for such a fourth year class was producing their own magazine. The teacher read them newspaper stories from local and tabloid press and showed them how they were constructed. Next there were discussion lessons, where news stories were improvised and interviews taped. Unconsciously many of the pupils mimicked the style of I.T.N. interviewers and of the "ordinary people" interviewed. They then wrote up the stories, based on incidents that had happened locally:

> TURKEY FARM RAIDED
>
> Yesterday a Buxted Turkey Farm was raided by an Animal Welfare Group. The manager and workers were stunned when the farm was attacked.
>
> The raid took place at a farm near Dalby. Around 80 turkeys were stolen and rags were stuffed up exhausts to stop people chasing them. The manager, a middle aged man was in at the time. When the group started the raid, the manager woke up and tried to ring the police, but the telephone lines had been cut.
>
> SURPRISE
>
> In an interview, the police said that the group had attacked because of the way the turkeys had been cooped up.
>
> The manager said that he was really surprised....

The boy who wrote this, Anthony, had been in Remedial classes or bottom sets all his career and in many schools it is quite likely that he would have been put in non-exam leavers' classes. Instead he was entered for C.S.E. He had definite criteria of attainment to aim at in a number of different subjects and an exam pass to work towards. He shows here his understanding of the format, vocabulary and tone of a local newspaper's front page story. A short paragraph summarising the story is followed by a lengthier explanation. There are two interviews. The first with the police is summarised. The second with the manager rather more detailed. Many of the standard phrases of T.V. and newspaper reporting are accurately caught: "stunned", "a middle aged man", "surprise". Anthony's work matured quite considerably during his last two years and he gained a range of C.S.E.'s including a Grade 3 C.S.E. in English.

Once a few pupils are able to understand the task and produce work of a sufficiently high standard, it can be read out to the class, copied out and mounted on the classroom walls. This provides a medium between the teacher, the original text and the rest of the class. It demonstrates how easy it is to write like a newspaperman, and it can quickly be adapted by slower, less able children. Terry, for instance, was rather a careless boy and left to his own devices he often produced rushed, superficial work. But with Anthony's article in mind, he produced a nicely timed satire:

> DRUNK RUNAWAYS
>
> Yesterday, three men in Mack Trucks rampaged around the County. They stole the brand new lorries and caused havoc.
>
> The three, all long distance lorry drivers are Mr Geof Sewell of 128 York Road, ...

Anthony and Terry's group all wrote main news stories, they visited the local magistrates' court and wrote Court Reports, they reviewed a play, video or pop concert. They wrote specialist articles on hobbies, topics of local interest, the stars or love stories. Eventually everyone in the class wrote a lengthy piece of prose of sufficiently high standard, which was corrected, copied up onto a duplicating sheet, printed and stapled up into a magazine. They were put on sale in the school and after the school materials were paid for, the profits were then divided among the group. This was a tremendous boost to the pupils' morale, and they were now seen to be capable, interesting and amusing writers.

Another way of enhancing self concepts is through media studies. Some Colleges of Education have film schools attached, and it is possible to mount a series of lessons about the way T.V. programmes are constructed. There are films which show how directors plan out their shooting scripts. On my P.G.C.E. course, a few students took groups of children into the College film studios, let them act in front of the cameras and mix the shots. Most Comprehensives now have access to video cameras, and some student teachers with a flair for dramas have got children with a history of learning difficulties to improvise their own dramas, film them and write them up afterwards.

With Anthony and Terry's group, we took a long

time to set up a suitable story. Paul had a joke box with a realistic plastic burn scar. He suggested that the play would be about children stealing acid and accidently spilling it on themselves. We improvised scenes in a pretend Chemistry lab, in another school room where the acid is dropped and in the Headmaster's office where the guilty boys and their mothers are summoned for the official punishment. A script was then knocked together on the basis of these improvisations.

We ran into a whole series of problems. Some of the teachers who were going to help out had to drop out, leading actors amongst the children were absent for vital rehearsals, and pupils forgot the script. But the advantage of working in video as opposed to film is that one can reshoot dud material. Posters were made and put up all round the school, advertising what a great movie this group had made. After the cost of the video tape had been reimbursed, the profits were sent off to a Blue Peter Appeal, which led to yet another mention in assembly for this group. Suddenly a vast range of children from the 'O' level classes to the top C.S.E. groups wanted to be in this set. The shooting scripts that all this work generated were some of the longest, most carefully put together and original that these pupils had ever done. Some wrote over 1000 words.

There are only a few students who have the confidence to attempt drama, especially anything as lengthy and as complex as this. Especially in schools where there is little tradition of drama, it can be quite hazardous. Children get over-excited, very noisy and difficult to control. Once in role, they won't come out. Fantasy and reality are harder to differentiate and it may take considerable acting skills on the part of the student teacher to reimpose his definition of the situation. So on a short teaching practice in schools which are unused to improvised drama, it's often best to be cautious and start with something fairly limited. Many plays have low readability levels and reading them is something that children with learning difficulties may enjoy. They can then be acted out, book in hand. The teacher then sets up a small scale domestic story, like a child arriving home very late and covered in mud or an adult trying to sell someone a second hand car. The "scripts" that result can be audio taped and then written up. Last of all one makes a one act video just for class consumption. This still raises morale and though it does not have the effect of a full scale movie, it removes the risks.

Some Colleges also operate M.S.C. Schemes where children's work can be typed out, illustrated and duplicated. This is another way that children with a history of learning difficulties can be persuaded to see themselves as writers. One can read to them pieces of literature that they would enjoy without necessarily being able to read themselves, excerpts from "Cider with Rosie" or Ted Hughes' "Pike", and then get them to write their own descriptive prose and poetry. One shows them how to make a second draft, correct their spelling and punctuation and sends it off to be printed. Copies of their own magazines can then be distributed round the school, given to friends, sold for charity and taken home to parents.

With one group we read poems from the Penguin "Animals" anthology, then observed a flock of seagulls paddling in the playground and tried to fit words to what we saw. The blackboard was soon covered with words, phrases and sections of verse about seagulls. Most of them wrote about seagulls but an imaginative eleven year old with a history of writing problems - from a poor script to gross inhibitions about putting pen to paper - came up with this poem about a "Hedgehog":

> Prickly and spiky,
> moves quite slowly
> catching flies with his sticky tongue.
> Curling up very tight
> When winter comes
> he's nowhere in sight
> he's hibernating under the leaves.
> There he snuggles up nice and warm.
> It's summer again
> he's in sight
> he's under the apple tree
> eating apples
> his little teeth munching away
> his little wet nose is so black.

Not only are poems like this appreciated by the children, the use of descriptive words and phrases makes their prose more vivid and sophisticated.

It is then possible for pupils with a history of learning difficulties to tackle writing tasks like a discursive essay or a literacy review, with considerable confidence. Robert, the boy whose critique of "Goalkeepers' Revenge" is shown below, came from a remote hill farm and as a child had hardly any friends to play with. His parents were very slow and inarticulate themselves, and Robert learned to talk late. He had special provision until the third year and even until the fifth year his smallness and timidity made him a natural victim for school bullies. It would not have been difficult for a boy like Robert to give up on school and like his hero, Spit Nolan, never come. Instead of which, he learned to write clear coherent essays with very few spelling or punctuation mistakes:

> Bill Naughton is the athor (sic). He was born in Ireland in 1910, afterwards his parents moved to England.
>
> He wrote the stories because he was on the dole in the years of the depression. He wrote stories for children about children. He wrote stories like Goalkeepers' Revenge and Spit Nolan. The stories were good and some were funny. The story about Spit Nolan is true.
>
> Spit Nolan had only one lung because he had lung disease. This disease couldn't be cured unless he went to Switzerland but Spit could not afford to. Spit never went to school and his pals envied him.

One can still see traces of Robert's learning difficulties.He misspells "author", though the word has been discussed in class and written on the blackboard many times. His handwriting is irregular and immature. He repeats words like "stories" and generally uses a restricted vocabulary. On the other hand, he understands how to shape his review, starting with a brief description of the man and his work, then setting the scene for the story he most enjoyed. And there is a sense of style and rhythm about his prose. The long sentence about Switzerland is followed with the simple but beautifully balanced:

> Spit never went to school and his pals envied him.

Robert eventually gained a range of C.S.E. passes including Grade 4 in English. His work represents one extreme in the spread of writing ability among school leavers with a history of learning difficulties. For students working in schools where there is no such emphasis on a continuity of meaningful writing tasks, this kind of achievement is almost incredible. Many pupils leave schools unable to write their addresses, compose a simple sickness note or fill in an application form. Being able to put together a simple road safety poster can be taxing for them. As a student teacher I once observed a Fourth year Easter Leaver, whose parents had moved fourteen times during his childhood and who had never been to the same school for two years running, copying from the blackboard in a Science lesson. He had so little idea of the meaning of the notes and of letter formation, he copied parts of words and parts of letters. Even with a boy like Herman, who had only two terms left to his schooling, it was possible, using the dictated experience approach, to get him to write something meaningful before leaving. He told us a story into a tape recorder, the story was transcribed and edited, so as to give him words he could read, and then he wrote it in his own handwriting.

This is not to argue that there is no place for exercises, either for Robert or for Herman. Both had problems with handwriting that regular practice could have alleviated. The problem for the teacher is to find ways in which this practice can be related to work that is meaningful and self motivating, especially when pupils might well have had years of "busywork" which has had little effect on them. With a wider audience in mind Robert, Anthony and Terry's group could be encouraged to use the experience of writing a magazine to take greater care with the minutiae. Where work is to be displayed or, even better, put on sale, it is surprising what a difference can be made. It is easier for the teacher to get pupils to have a look at what makes their writing unattractive or difficult to read. It may be that the child is poorly coordinated and his writing is unpredictable and irregular. Even here, it is possible to get the pupil to copy up a story on wide lined paper and then go over it with him, getting him to spot which letters drift over the line, which are bigger than others, which too small, which upstrokes lean to the right, which to the left. Some teachers then go over the letters in coloured pen "correcting" them, before getting the pupil to do the same. This sensitizes the pupils to what makes his writing difficult to read, and gives him something to aim at.

Most children do not have these gross physical

difficulties. Their problem is not that they have poor control over hands and fingers, rather that they learned to form letters wrongly. "u" and "n" might be written with the same indeterminate rising stroke, "a" is not joined at the top and so looks like "u", "t" might go uncrossed. Here one might want to target a few letters, select the right handwriting exercises from a programme and get the child to practice those of his letters which most confuse the reader. The targets can be written at the back of the English book and then the pupil "corrects" the letters concerned before handing in each piece of work.

Normally it is extremely difficult to achieve any long term improvement in the handwriting of secondary age pupils. One may give them handwriting lessons, but unless the pupils themselves want to change, there is little long term effect. Habits stick, a script seems to express personality and even though the children feel they ought to improve, they soon slip back into old ways. One way of dramatizing the problem is for the teacher to print out one child's story for duplication, omitting those letters which cause him most difficulty. The story is then distributed as a cloze analysis. The pupils have to make sense of the story by filling in the appropriate letters. Sometimes very able children with handwriting problems come to a Special Needs base. Simple injunctions to write more neatly have had no effect, they may even have learned an alternative script which is just too slow and cumbersome for everyday use. A simple explanation of the way adults use "cues" to guess at the phrases they are reading, plus a cloze analysis of their own work can give them a clearer understanding of what they should be aiming at.

Given the fillip of having their work "published", handwriting can be turned into a positive concern for the child. If a class begins to feel that one person's untidiness lets them all down, they will then exert group pressure. One can then see rapid changes. Everyone now writes the date above each piece of work, underlines the title, uses a range of coloured inks and so on. And then one sees that children who have had problems for years keeping their writing on the line suddenly achieving this. Handwriting is now seen as the medium through which something worthwhile is produced, rather than the occasion for rebukes.

Many teachers of children with Special Needs

see spelling as a distinct subject. This is particularly true of those who use the diagnostic approach to reading. Children with spelling difficulties are envisaged as having underlying perceptual or conceptual problems. They divide all poor spellers into three groups : those with visual perception difficulties, those with aural perception problems and those with a weak understanding of spelling rules and patterns. A child with visual perceptual difficulties can divide a word up into syllables and spell each phonetically. But he cannot "see" it and so makes simple errors. If you ask them to spell a word like "pieces" out loud, a child with visual difficulties may even sound the letters correctly. Yet they may have just written it as "PECIES" in a story and not be able to "see" the mistake until it is pointed out to them. One of the most intelligent partially sighted pupils I have met had problems of this kind. Despite an IQ of over 120, there was a time when it appeared unlikely he would be entered for 'O' level, so poor was his spelling. That is not to say, however, that all partially sighted children spell badly or that other pupils with good sight make these kinds of error. One meets lots of other children who "know" a sequence of letters when asked to spell it out loud, yet who cannot spot a sequencing mistake in their work. Quite a few remedial teachers using the diagnostic approach will embark on lengthy programmes which include the sequencing of objects, symbols and nonsense syllables, the use of multisensory techniques like "writing" words in the air or on sandpaper.

A few children, especially those who learned to read very late, have problems with basic letter/sound correspondences, and will even confuse i/e, a/e and some consonants. And yet they can write larger more difficult words more easily. The remedial teacher might say these children have excellent visual memories but that that aural memory is impaired. They will set up programmes which differentiate every day household sounds like a kettle whistling and a door squeaking on its hinges, then move onto letter sounds. Schemes like "Alpha to Omega" (Hornsby and Shear) are used for dictation exercises.It is most important the child has his own dictionary of spelling keywords, the basic building blocks which make a piece of prose difficult to read. These target words are practised, revised and tested until they are mastered.

The third group of children may well be able to translate letter/sound correspondences and "see" letter sequences correctly, but they do not know the spelling patterns or rules. In some cases, this may well be because they have such limited reading experience, they have not quite fixed all the words in their oral vocabulary. A child with a history of reading difficulties who has only read a few plays may write "Sceen One". He knows there is a "See" in the word, and that this is not an "ea" word, but he has not quite got the letter order right. There are also pupils who are highly intelligent and will read widely, who have not grasped the doubling rules or understood the way that Latinate prefixes shape the spelling of words like "disappear". This third group are thought to have "conceptual" or "lexical" difficulties.

Some lecturers, especially those particularly concerned with the spelling problems of highly intelligent "dyslexic" children, get their students to bring the work that their students have received from their pupils for spelling diagnosis in College. Except in very extreme cases, much of the evidence for this kind of visual/aural/conceptual analysis is highly ambiguous, though and for the last thirty years there have been fierce arguments about the effectiveness of a diagnostic approach. Highly individualised spelling programmes used in one-to-one teaching tend to break down with classes of 15 or more. Those linguists who are sceptical about dyslexia would maintain that all spelling is about patterns and rules, so all spelling problems are conceptual, anyway (Chomsky). All children should have their personalised spelling dictionaries, all children should be encouraged to check and sound out the words they are unsure of and all children should be taught the underlying rules of Latinate prefixes and doubling.

Faced with a mixed ability class which includes children with a range of spelling difficulties, an occasional half term burst with a published programme like "Basil Blackwell" (Stockdale) should keep most children progressing. One tests the children, finds a spelling age and uses this to determine the level at which children should start. There are rule cards every now and again to emphasise spelling patterns. Most children will get most of the words right, they mark their own work and the scheme is self motivating. Schemes like this often bring about rapid short term gains in most children, especially when measured against the spelling age. Even so, the long term effects for others are fairly limited. The pupils learn the rules, do the exercises and then make precisely the same errors in their next story. One needs to follow up a spelling programme with an attempt to make spelling a positive everyday affair, something that relates to their writing and reading.

It could be argued that what distinguishes children with spelling problems is that they do not make use of checking mechanisms. The relationship between what a pupil really "knows" when he is on the look out for his own spelling errors and what can be taught is immensely complex. A child learns how to spell from a myriad sources. He picks up a lot just through seeing the word often enough in his books, comics, through advertising hoardings and T.V. Many children are given lists of spellings to learn throughout primary school, week in week out, with little attempt to relate the spelling patterns that underline them. Some rules are learned and then misapplied. "Eye before Ee" can generate "receive" and "wiegh". Some visual patterns are confused with letter/sound correspondences and words like "seid" are learned wrong. Such anomalies provide yet another twist to the complexity of English spelling for those who think of it as difficult, anyway.

As most successful spellers write, they "know" from the feel of the pen and the look of the word whether it is coming out right. An experienced typist "knows" whether a word is typed correctly even though she does not look at what she is typing. If we have any doubts, we focus on a word, think about it more deeply, write it out on scrap paper or go for the dictionary. The poor speller, however, may feel so helpless that he does not even have any confidence about his doubts. He may even be afraid to ask the teacher because he does not want to show himself up in class.

If one is dealing with a large class which contains pupils with spelling difficulties it can be a great deal of good to emphasise that the way most of us learn to spell new words is to admit that we are unsure. Even teachers need a dictionary to check their own work from time to time. We all feel embarrassed at being caught out, so there are to be no funny cracks about anybody else's spelling problems. Any pupil is allowed to ask a question about how any word is spelt from "as", "any" and "table" to "ethyl" and "parliamentary." At first a mixed ability group will probably come up with difficult words, but as they become more trusting they then check up on easy ones. A child who asks for "said", may copy it from the board correctly at first, but then go back to "seid", so at the end of a lesson the class is asked to check their spellings against the words on the blackboard.

As the teacher gets to know what kinds of problems the children have, he can encourage the use of "long" words. He will tell some children to guess at the word, put it on a scrap of paper and bring it up to him for checking. Those few children whose misspellings are markedly "visual", "aural" or "conceptual" can be told that they seem to have such a problem and shown how to use other strategies to check their work. When a poor speller is seated next to a good speller, when they are friends and there is no shame in asking for help they can be told to try helping each other. Sooner or later some of the good spellers in the class will feel that they are missing out on the teachers' attention. They will shout out the words that others have asked the teacher for. It must be emphasised that spelling is a matter between those who ask and those who are asked. There is no shame in not knowing a spelling, only in not asking when one was not sure. Whether we "know" a spelling or not, we all know whether we have doubts about it. These doubts should not weigh us down, they should put us to work. When such an approach becomes part of our everyday writing lessons, particularly when it becomes part of our work across the curriculum, the pupils relax and become more positive. It may not have the short term successes of the one to one diagnostic and teaching programmes of Dyslexic Institutes or of the programmed approaches, but it can complement these in the long term, and it is much less time consuming.

Poor spelling and handwriting can obscure the meaning of a piece of writing and so hinder communication. Just as much a problem is sentence structure. Some children with a history of learning difficulties may not seem to understand that spoken language has a structure, that it has its pauses, emphases and sense of shape. Backward readers with a reading age of less than 8.5 may well be used to reading books which use line lengths to echo these conversational pauses and different colour print to mark out speech. They may be so concerned to sound out each word correctly they read so haltingly that the sense of a phrase or sentence or whole paragraph may not mean much to them. So when it comes to writing, they have very few mental cues as to where to put full stops, capital letters, speech marks and new paragraphs.

One response adopted in many classrooms is to teach children the "rules" and then give them sentences, chosen virtually at random, which they then have to punctuate. Pupils will sit for lesson after lesson, quietly copying these exercises out, putting full stops at the beginning, commas between lists, speech marks round speech and full stops at the end. Yet when they write their next story they make exactly the same errors.

Another approach is to attempt to model the conventions of written grammar on the conventions of speech. One way round this is to get children to tell a story out loud without using "And", "But" or "Then". These conjunctions are widely used as "markers" in oral story telling. They show that the speaker has not finished, whilst giving him time to think of what comes next. Depriving a child who is not aware of conversational structures but who is a good story teller of his "And then's" can be quite traumatic. How can one keep the listeners' attention ? The rhythm of the story goes awry and the overall structure of the story seems to break down. It's at this point that the teacher can point out that in a written story this is where the full stop should go. Learning not to use "and then" becomes an oral game. The children with pronounced problems in sentence structure sit in a circle, trying to see how long they can keep going without bringing one in. Eventually when the group has mastered that, children whose writing is rather banal can be brought into the circle and the story is then told in sentences which start with "When ..." "If ..." and "Although ..."

When the group has got the idea, it can be transferred into written work. The "rule" can be emphasised before children set to work, the use of more complex sentences mentioned once they have got into their stories and then at the end the class can be asked to check what they have written. A similar approach can be adopted towards the use of speech marks. First a small scale drama can be set up, then the "speeches" can be taped and transcribed, then the speech can be punctuated on the blackboard and lastly the rules of speech marks can be deduced. When the pupils seem to have appreciated the basic principles through Oral lessons, comic strip cartoons and so on, they can be asked to include dialogue in their stories. It is astonishing how impressive this can make a three section story: the first paragraph the setting of the scene, the second a properly punctuated conversation and the third a conclusion.

After a few such lessons, children with a history of learning difficulties can produce something which satisfies the criteria of external exams - a bravura exhibition of commas and quotation marks - and also captures the rhythms of real conversation.

A few teachers will start in schools where the demands of an external exam are thought to be too great or irrelevant for children who have had a history of learning difficulties, but which nevertheless believe that if pupils made their own folders of written work, this gives them something with which to impress employers. Some teachers from Swindon found that this greatly improved standards of written work. Unfortunately a Schools Council review (Swales) discovered that employers still wanted to know what these meant in terms of 'O' levels and C.S.E.'s and assumed that those who were without external exams were failures. The same has been said about the use of profiles for non-exam pupils. Nevertheless as this Schools Council research suggested, the overall effect on pupil motivation was encouraging, despite their eventual disappointment.

It could be argued that in those few schools where pupils with a history of learning difficulties take and pass C.S.E.'s the fact that the grades are generally restricted to 4's and 5's underlines the fact that the pupils are still at the bottom of the heap. Furthermore being able to write a literary review on "The Goalkeeper's Revenge" or a discursive essay on "Animals and Society" is hardly relevant to the kind of life that pupils like Robert, Anthony or Terry see for themselves. This is a complex area, where there are no easy answers. One response would be that providing the writing was grounded in the more relevant skills of reading, talking and listening, and providing that they were on exam courses which made them feel that they were doing the same as everybody else, then these kinds of essays, stories and plays could be as worthwhile. At present, criteria for a Grade 4 English C.S.E. are that:

> Work should show the rudiments of language competence. In general the candidate can communicate in spite of inaccuracies. His

work is redeemed by descriptive touches.

It may well seem astonishing that after eleven years of schooling even those with a history of learning difficulties could not use "writing" to "communicate". This is, one would argue, not merely a function of the pupils' intellectual or linguistic problems, but a product of a mechanical approach to writing across the curriculum, a lack of consistent teaching and an emphasis on the remediation of inaccuracies at the expense of communication still seen in far too many Comprehensive Schools.

REFERENCES

Chomsky, C. (1971) Reading Writing and Phonology: Harvard Ed. Review 40 : 287-309

Furlong, V. (1977) Anancy Goes to School: a Case Study in Pupils' Knowledge of Their Teachers in School Experience Ed. Woods, P. and Hammersley, M. : Croom Helm

Hornsby, B. and Shear, F. (1976) Alpha to Omega : Heinemann

Stockdale, W. (1978) Talk Write and Spell : Basil Blackwell

Sharp, R. and Green, A. (1975) Education and Social Control : Routledge

Swales, T. (1979) Record of Personal Achievement : Schools Council

FURTHER READING

Cotterell, G. (1969) Check List of Basic Sound L.D.A

English 5-16 (1984) HMI Discussion Paper : HMSO

Frith, U. (1980) Cognitive Processes in Spelling: Academic Press

Holbrook, D. (1964) English for the Rejected : C.U.P

Miles, T.R. (1970): On Helping the Dyslexic Child: Methuen

Peters M.L. (1967) Spelling Caught or Taught : Routledge

Chapter Five

MATHS AS A MEANS OF COMMUNICATION

At the start of my own P.G.C.E. course, a visit was arranged by the College to an inner-city Comprehensive, which boasted an innovative humanities curriculum project. The headmaster assured us that we were free to visit any part of the school, so long as staff were forewarned, and so last period in the afternoon I sat in on a Maths lesson. The class were "Easter leavers", fourth year bottom set, who were meant to be following a practical course. The teacher had on his desk two piles of text books. The first was a set of practical problems, the second mechanical arithmetic. When I arrived, the teacher had just given out the first pile. It appeared that the pupils were expected to work through the books at their own pace. The teacher seemed very ill prepared to manage such a complex operation. He had not marked the books recently. He did not know which children were tackling which problem. He had not anticipated the difficulties they might run into.

Most children reacted as if they had no clear idea of what they were supposed to be doing. The teacher had given his opening explanation, but instead of repeating it some other way, he just barked at them to get on with their work. A few actually opened their books and began to write, but the rest just flicked through them calling out, "What page we on?" The teacher grew more and more exasperated, until he burst out in a furious lecture about how if they could not manage this Practical Maths they would have to do sums again. He collected the problems for school leavers and passed out the mechanical exercises. Paradoxically, the class now settled down; they even seemed to enjoy covering pages of their exercise book with these straightforward additions and subtractions.

This observation was at least as valuable as that of the humanities curriculum project. One was seeing the more mundane and perhaps more chilling problems that teachers have in educating less able pupils. For the first and more ambitious part of his lesson, the teacher was barely in control of his class. He had certainly communicated nothing of Maths to them. Even at the most basic level, he had not even thought out what it was he expected them to learn. He assumed that his class could simply manage to develop their own understanding through reading textbooks and carrying out written examples. But worst of all there seemed to be no rapport between teacher and taught. The only communication between them was what book and what exercises the class should do.

There is tremendous variation in the teaching of Maths to children with Special Needs. In some schools all the members of the Maths Department take turns with the least able. The Head of Department covers the whole age range over a period of years, to ensure he has an overview of the whole syllabus. But quite a few operate on the principle of "horses for courses". Teachers with the greatest experience, the better degrees and proven skill are reserved for 'O' and 'A' level teaching, whilst those who are fresh from College, or whose discipline is poor, or who have a non-specialist qualification take the less able groups. Remedial departments often take responsibility for bottom Maths sets, even though few Special Needs staff have Maths degrees or specialist training. They often feel insecure teaching more advanced mathematical concepts so they stick to mechanical arithmetic. The Cockcroft Committee (1982) reported as a result that: "Syllabuses can sometimes be excessively narrow".

It is quite possible for children with learning difficulties to spend a considerable proportion of their secondary career practising sums they were first taught in Infants school and yet leave school without a basic understanding of numbers.

They also have problems with the practical skills of money, time or measurement and the mathematics of proportion, ratio, algebra and geometry. Well taught throughout their school career, it is quite possible for children with a history of learning difficulties to follow an exam course, which includes all these topics and others covered in the Cockcroft Committee's list of

Foundation Skills: percentages, use of calculator, graphs and pictorial representation and statistical ideas. (see Cockcroft : para 458).

Just as teaching skills differ markedly in this area, so do the abilities of the children. Despite the attraction of fine streaming to many Maths Departments, bottom streams are not always what they appear. Some are used to catering for those with learning difficulties in Maths, as well as far more able children who refuse to work or are disruptive. A very few of these may have IQ's in the superior range. One girl was transferred from a "good" C.S.E. set to the bottom group because she was a nuisance and because she had missed so many of her Maths lessons during the exam term of her third year. The reason she was absent was because she had been attending a family therapy unit. The psychologist thought that one of the reasons she had been disruptive in Maths was because she was bored. The work was insufficiently demanding and it had been recommended that she be promoted to an 'O' level set.

At the opposite extreme there may be children whose reading and writing are poor but who can just about cope with the literary demands of the school - and yet whose problems with Maths are considerably greater than the rest of the Maths set. One occasionally comes across children with a reading age of seven and who can add to 10, but who have no grasp of subtraction, time or measurement. Two such children, the boy called James, whose E.T. story was mentioned in the previous chapter and a girl called Yvonne who was later transferred to a Special School, entered Secondary School able to count to 100 and carry out written addition sums, but neither had a clear grasp of concepts like "bigger" or "more than". They could do the sum 5 + 3 = 8 but were at a loss if you asked them, "What number is three more than five ?" The main reason that Yvonne went to the Special School was that her reading and writing were poor and she had made no progress in the Secondary School. The majority of children who transfer to Special Schools from Junior or Secondary Schools are selected because of problems in reading, writing and behaviour, hardly any because of exceptional problems in Maths.

Given the range of abilities and attitudes one is likely to meet in bottom Maths sets or the Special Needs classes of ordinary schools, it is clear that effective teaching will depend on careful assessment. Assessment for Special Needs could be seen as a threefold process. Firstly one wants a rough idea of where each of the children fits into the overall distribution of ability. For this one needs a norm referenced test. Secondly one wants a test that will cover a range of topics and analyse each into skills and operations. This requires a criterion referenced test. Thirdly one needs to evaluate how particular children learn, what helps them overcome their difficulties and what they might be capable of, given special treatment or adaptions to existing syllabuses and resources. For this one needs practical, informal or classbased assessment.

Even before one enters the classroom it may be illuminating to look at the way Maths tests are constructed and the issues they raise for teachers of children with Special Needs. Some students have taken some of the findings of the Assessment of Performance Unit on place value and the first four functions, and then generated tests of their own. One can then look at the topics Special Needs staff cover in greater detail. One workshop group developed a list of over 60 criteria of the ability to add. This enabled them to appreciate that even the most thorough tests have an element of selection and that some of the errors which pupils with Special Needs make are not accounted for. The fullest and best constructed formal test may or may not pinpoint particular areas of difficulty in individual children.

Global scores on an in-school end of term exam may well mask quite marked differences in skill or understanding. Some of the children in Special Needs sets might be of average ability in mechanical arithmetic and in their handling of money, yet be quite poor in measurement, drawing or geometry.

Johnny, for example, had always had problems with numbers. When he arrived at the Comprehensive School he would make silly mistakes if asked to add numbers like 8 + 3 or subtract 5 from 11. Since arithmetic had been the staple of his Junior School curriculum, this left him with little faith in his abilities. Later on he learned how to use a calculator and this relieved many of his anxieties. By the middle of the third year, he had a standardized score of just below 90 in addition and subtraction in a norm referenced test. That is to say, in comparison with all the other children of his age in the country, he was only slightly below average. Yet in geometry he was very quick to catch on. He could measure angles, differentiate between perimeters and areas and he grasped concepts like that when straight lines intersect, opposite pairs of angles are equal. Criteria referenced tests or profiles which differentiated spatial and arithmetical understanding had indicated these differences quite clearly, and these would have been useful to a teacher working through these different topics with him. What criteria referenced tests would not show up, however, was that if you gave Johnny a calculator and asked him to divide all the numbers between 1 and 10 by 8, he would fail to "see" the pattern:

0.125
0.25
0.375
0.5
0.625
0.75
0.875
1 etc.

He would laboriously work through the set unable to predict what was coming next.

It is only when one begins to teach children with learning difficulties that one begins to appreciate the limitations of written test data. There are many reasons why children fail and John Holt has shown more vividly than most how much underachievement in Maths stems from the teachers' incomprehension of the way children make sense of the subject to themselves. For the able mathematician, Maths may well have an aesthetic appeal, an imaginative attraction and a clarity that goes beyond words. Getting the less able to appreciate these qualities requires considerable skill. For the child who already feels a failure, Maths can be more sinister than any other form of knowledge, cold, unreal and obscure. Lacking confidence, he may withdraw from the lesson,dream, make infantile guesses and silly errors. The effective teacher needs to know much more than where the child is "up to" in the syllabus, how he compares with his peers and what skills he can demonstrate on paper. In order to get the best of children with difficulties in the subject, he must understand the processes the child uses to make sense of a topic. One of the best ways of doing this is through interaction with small groups of pupils. It is through the recording of how pupils communicate their understanding of a topic that the teacher realizes how to teach, what to reinforce and how to raise their expectations.

Transcriptions of conversations between pupils with learning difficulties and their teachers can be brought into College to show how one can make these informal assessments. The following is taken from a geometry lesson. A small group is studying the properties of parallel lines. They have drawn parallel lines with rulers and set squares. Now they have drawn another line across the parallels and measured the angles it makes.

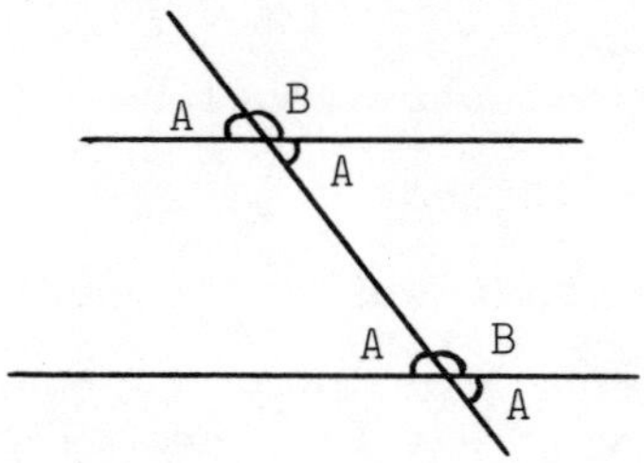

After measuring quite a few sets of angles, this small group began to realize that all the angle A's were the same. Furthermore angle A plus angle B was always 180°. They then tested their hypotheses with another drawing and began to talk about why this should be, and how they could predict B from A.

Curly: Four sides (i.e. angles) are 70° and one is 110°, so the rest must be 110°.

Teacher: Why do you think that is, Curly? You are absolutely right. Well done. Now why do you think it is?

Curly: Cos the rest is 70° ... and I just thought the rest might be 110°.

Teacher: You're quite right.

Martin: When you say one is 110° all the rest must be 110° as well.

Teacher: They should indeed, but why?

Curly: Cos they're all parallel lines.

Teacher: Cos they're all parallel lines. Good. Fantastic.

Fred: Both 110° and ... are on the same point on the protractor.

Teacher: Both 70° and 110° are on the same point on the protractor ... So?

Fred: So if you add them up they add up to 180° and that's a straight line.

Teacher: And why do all those angles add up to 180°?

Arthur: They're all straight lines.

Teacher: They are indeed.

It becomes clear that while the pupils have begun to digest the properties of two straight lines intersecting, and that they have found a very speedy and effective way of predicting angle B from angle A, they have not yet begun to understand why the angles on the top line should be the same as those on the bottom. It was just "Cos they're all parallel lines". Having made the discovery that if angle A was 70°, angle B must be 110°, Curly's confidence collapsed and he could not see why this must be so. It took Fred to make the connection with 180° and Arthur to see that both angles "added up" to a "straight line". As the group explains its discoveries to one another, it helps them to understand them, to relate them to other mathematical ideas, to perceive patterns - and in doing so it helps the teacher to understand how much of his lesson they have understood. Even with this opportunity for praise, it's not difficult for children to lose confidence, to lose the thread and become confused.

James, the child whose E.T. story was described in the last chapter, was very easily disheartened. The dreaming, which was so useful to him in writing imaginative stories, seemed to undermine his concentration in Maths. He was solidly convinced he would never learn anything. At the end of the first term, though, the group was introduced to the school's computers. His brother had a "Spectrum" too, and he knew what the teacher was doing. When it was his turn for "hands on" he was quicker than anyone else. The next lesson, the class were shown how a home made addition and subtraction programme could be used to take the tedium out of practice, and he knew how to recall programs and make alterations in them. His enthusiasm spilled over into his attempting the sums and he began to change from a child who avoided all kinds of teacher questions to one who was prepared to relax and take risks. The computer lessons marked a watershed in terms of his attitude to Maths and we noticed how much more alert and positive he became afterwards. Previously it was as if James spent all his energy defending himself against the subject. He resisted all attempts to stir his interest or involvement. Now there was a part of Maths he knew he could succeed in, the whole subject appeared less threatening.

This enabled us to make faster progress in teaching him his number bonds. In extreme cases like his, where children's grasp of arithmetic is very limited and appears to rest on mechanical skills, teachers of slow learners often find it necessary to recapitulate the whole sequence of developmental learning stages. They would argue that if a child has learned a set of discrete number facts like 7 + 2 = 9 or 9 - 2 = 7, but has no idea of what number is two less than nine or what number you need to add to seven to make nine, it may be that he has formed an insufficient understanding of what the basic numbers correspond to in terms of feel, touch or visual patterns. One starts with the sensory - motor stage, where one learns through touch, feel and rhythm. The teacher and pupil count on their fingers, tap out the rhythms of 3, 4,and 5, count to 10, count to six, count to five. They show what each number looks like in turn. They then take what for a few children can be a tremendous leap. They are asked to produce a set of four fingers all at once, a set of six, a set of nine, without counting them out sequentially.

The next stage would be to count out objects, plastic blocks or coins, then to make patterns of those objects. The child then begins to associate the pattern itself with the number, rather than the objects so grouped. He can now draw a 6 pattern and a 4 pattern, recognise the pattern on dice or dominoes. One can then make flashcards to reinforce the number patterns and gradually build up speed and accuracy. Children like James might have been taught these patterns before in Infants School, have been given apparatus to make number patterns and have copied seven ducks and seven cups, coloured in pages of examples and finished the workbook without ever grasping the arithmetical structures that underlay these visual patterns.

When they passed onto sums, they would have had little understanding of the relationships between numbers. They would not have had a very clear visual image of 5, so they would not have realised that this is the number that is two more than three, two less than seven, half of ten and so on.

When one begins to revise addition with a child like James, one has to show that three is two more than one, four is two more than two, five is two more than three; firstly by counting on fingers, then by showing sets of fingers, then through counters and coins and drawings, until at last he is fast and accurate at adding all the numbers below 10 orally and without the assistance of objects. The process then starts again for graded examples of subtraction:

> 3 less than 3, 3 less than 4, three taken from 5, you have six pennies, then take 3 away and so on.

Progress might be very slow at first but gradually, as the child begins to understand the conceptual structures behind the number bonds, the rate of acquisition begins to speed up.Only when the teacher is quite sure that the child can communicate his understanding orally, can he give him written examples. It took James almost half a year to get to this stage. Very occasionally one comes across 15 or 16 year olds who have not reached it and who cannot progress beyond the most basic forms of mechanical arithmetic. It can take even longer to teach them and relieve them of their crushing anxieties.

Even within a small Special Needs group, it was obvious that James' needs were quite distinct from those of the rest. It was necessary to organize lessons very thoroughly in advance at a number of different levels. Supposing the rest of the class was being taught volume, the first part of the lesson was arranged as a practical demonstration, so that James could be included in it. Then James would be set a task he could manage on his own, while the basic principles of capacity were explained to the rest. They would then be set a task to get on with individually or in small groups. They would be told to work quietly so that the teacher could now give James his undivided attention. The normal distractions that a class employs as it settles to work - one child unsure of an exercise, another lacking pens or pencils, a third looking out of the window, others starting a quarrel - all of these had to be foreseen and dealt with in advance. Then James would be seated in such a way that the teacher could work with him and survey the whole of the rest of the class. Finally, James' work would have to be organised in such a way that he could carry on without help, so that as the rest of the class finished their activity the teacher could check their work to see how well they had understood.

Gradually, as James mastered his number bonds, it became easier to include him in more of the topics the rest were studying. One still had to beware of the questions in the textbook. The readability level might be too high or they might be too difficult for him mathematically. One would have to adapt a written exercise or set him an individualised work card. Eventually he caught up with some of the rest and one merely had to ensure that he had extra opportunities for discussion. Without his sudden and public success in the computer lessons, however, he might well have lacked the will to make this slow and steady progress.

There are times when every teacher feels that he or she is teaching a group nothing, whatever the subject or whatever the apparent ability level. When one starts teaching children who have experienced years of failure and discouragement, it is easy to let the pupils' sense of hopelessness affect one's teaching. A colleague with considerable experience of teaching reading and Arts subjects, but who was taking her first Maths group, used to say that the children were enjoying her lessons well enough but that their Maths seemed to be getting worse. This may be because of the way the syllabus was arranged, because of the way the exercises are graded or even because of unforeseen difficulties with materials or equipment. Despite its considerable advantages, even the calculator can present problems as we shall see. In this colleague's case, part of the difficulty was that the textbook she was using was designed for much younger average ability children and there were a range of unexpected pitfalls. If one blindly follows a textbook with a bottom Maths set, failure can occur with heartless regularity.

Learning how to spot areas of potential difficulty as one is preparing a lesson is crucial. Assessment data may be of some help. This becomes clear if one looks at measurement. Children who have not achieved mastery of place value up to 1000 will need a considerable amount of support when learning about kilograms. That is not to say children should not study weight until they are at home with 1000's. The practice with the first can be used to develop understanding of the second. But it may well be that a textbook or set of workcards the teacher is following were not written with the needs of such children in mind. The topic may well start promisingly enough, with practice in estimation, but one can run into difficulties almost before one knows it. Pupils may begin by holding a weight from a grocer's balance in one hand, and balance it against a book, a bag of sugar or a piece of chalk. They then put the objects in the balance. It may take some practice until they begin to realise that the size of something does not always give a very reliable indication as to weight. Quite a large stone from the garden may weigh less than a fisherman's lead sinker, and learning to let the muscles in the arm relax and feel the strain is quite an art. Next the book might demonstrate the way that a Salter weighing machine works, with the metal spring taking the strain in exactly the same way. Lastly, they use a modern electronic machine, with a display just like in the supermarket.

For the writers of many Maths books the next logical step is to reunite the concept of scale with the first four functions. As a result children are asked to add together the weights of objects, to multiply them, to divide in half and so on. The examples involve whole and half kilograms, and hundreds and tens of grams. Unless very thoroughly prepared, many of the children in the bottom Maths set will not know how to set out a sum like:

700 gm + 20 gm =

They may write:

$$\begin{array}{r} 700 \\ + \underline{\quad 20} \end{array} \quad \text{or even} \quad \begin{array}{l} 700 \\ +\underline{20\ \ } \end{array} \quad\quad \begin{array}{r} 700 \\ + \underline{\quad 20} \end{array}$$

Though they may well have learned that 1kg = 1000gms they will not find it easy to use that information in the sum: 1kg + 700gms

They may write:

$$\begin{array}{r} 1 \\ +\ \underline{700} \end{array} \quad \text{or} \quad \begin{array}{l} 1 \\ +\ \underline{700} \end{array}$$

Finally, it is not uncommon for textbooks to deal with weight immediately after length. Children with poor reading comprehension confuse kilometres, kilograms, metres, centimetres and grams, and expect there to be 100 grams in a kilogram. Such pupils have no way of checking the answers to their sums. 1 kg of sugar added to 100 gms of sweets may be written as:

$$\begin{array}{r} 1 \\ +\ \underline{100} \end{array} \quad \text{or} \quad \begin{array}{l} 1000 \\ +\ \underline{100\ \ } \end{array} \quad \text{or} \quad \begin{array}{r} 100 \\ +\ \underline{100} \end{array} \quad \text{or} \quad \begin{array}{r} 1000 \\ +\ \underline{\ \ 100} \end{array}$$

and any of the answers may appear to be reasonable.

Overcoming such difficulties may involve a critical look at a whole term's syllabus. At the beginning of the term, for instance, one may want to revise place value, to ensure that children remember about thousands, hundreds, tens and units and the importance of putting the right number in the right column. Secondly, one may want to give the class practice in setting out addition and subtraction sums "sideways", before setting them out in thousands, hundreds, tens and units columns. Thirdly one may want to weave into one's other topics as many practical activities involving 10's, 100's and 1000's as one can. For instance, in lessons on money, one can make piles of coins, to show what 100p looks like. One can show how thick a pile of £1 notes make £10 and estimate what £100 or £1000 would look like. The £1000 pile can be renamed a kilo-pound to reinforce the notion that kilo means 1000. This game caught the imagination of one class who wanted to know what a million pounds would look like in a single stack. We found out that the Cockcroft Report had 310 pages - or 155 pieces of paper - and that it measured 1.7 cm. Presuming that a banknote is about the same thickness as a page of Cockcroft, we estimated that £1550 was about 17 cm thick, £1,550,000 was about 17000 cm and £1m was just over 100m. We could see the running track out of the school's window and decided that laid on their side, the notes would cover the sprint section. In a single pile one on top of each other, they would be as tall as a skycraper over 30 storeys high - much taller than the tallest building in the nearest city. Pictures of some of these piles of money could then be put up in the classroom as a permanent visual reminder of the relative sizes of large numbers.

When one comes to the exercises in weight one may have to rewrite them both in terms of the objects at hand and the kinds of place value problems they present. One starts, perhaps by adding together 10's of gms from an old school chemical balance, estimating answers before checking them on the electronic machine, then going on to 100's of gms. One then gives a quick reminder of the place value lessons before mixing 10's and 100's. Only then can one move onto kgms and 100's. Concentration and motivation may still be high enough to give a group written exercises without the practical equipment. It is quite possible, however, that by now the group has had enough of this topic, are bored and want to move on. One then has to decide whether to complete the topic there and then, as the textbook suggests, or whether to give the group time to digest this new knowledge and come back to weight later. If a series of lessons go very well and a group does seem to be picking up a lot and enjoying their Maths, it is tempting to brush aside these signs of satiety.

With another group, for instance, we were coming to the end of a very successful series of lessons on factors, when they signalled they had had enough. We had done a thorough revision of tables, division and long division, at the beginning of all three terms. We had done an earlier chapter on factors, and prime numbers, carefully learning out the section on multiples to avoid a well known area of confusion. The children knew that the factors of 12 were 2, 6, 3 and 4. They could also find out the factors of larger numbers using estimation and calculators.

$$169 \div 7 = 24.142$$
$$169 \div 9 = 18.777$$
$$169 \div 11 = 15.363$$
$$169 \div 13 = 13$$

They also knew how to work out simple primes in the same way. The later chapter in this textbook took us back over this material and then introduced the concept of a prime factor. The group seemed thoroughly confused by the idea. Their grasp on the difference between primes and factors was still so new that this attempt to bring the two terms together made them feel muddled. Also instead of giving lots of simple problems the exercise quickly went on to large numbers. They also felt they had had enough of factors. I was sure they could just complete this last section. (Being able to do it would get them good marks in the common exam at the end of the year!). As a result, the very last lesson on this section of the course gave them the feeling that factors were difficult and that a little temporary success had finished in yet another failure. It is not always easy to spot these kinds of problems in advance, or to interpret the feedback one gets from a class, but it is essential if one is to continue communicating mathematics to children with a history of learning difficulties. Teaching these children seems to involve more than sensitive assessment, instances of success and the provision of an appropriate curriculum. The very interconnectedness of the subject has to communicate itself and ideally one wants the child to realize the interconnectedness of his or her own successes in it.

For Julia there seemed no end to her insecurity. Whatever topic we were looking at she would sit bemused and silent during the practical work and discussions and then get her first half dozen written examples wrong. She would add when she was supposed to subtract, forget number bonds and produce bizarre answers. She gradually gained in confidence in her first two years but Maths still seemed stale and impossible. One of her favourite sayings was, "We did that at Junior School. I didn't understand it then and I don't understand it now." If one tried to explain an idea slowly and patiently from first principles she quickly gave up. If you gave her a ritual she could follow and always get her sums right, she said she did not "get it". This written account gives the impression of an impossibly sour and ungracious girl, with an unhappy experience in Primary School. In fact she was sweet-tempered and her relations with her previous teachers were very positive. It was just that Maths lessons made her feel especially helpless.

Julia expected all kinds of problems with fractions and decimals. A calculator helped her to "do" decimals but she still suspected she did not understand them. Eventually, through looking back at pie charts with 1/10's and 1/100's sections and realizing that the calculator was merely turning up commonsense answers, she had the confidence to attempt the addition and subtraction of decimals without the calculator. Extra homework practice and parental encouragement made her as adept as the rest of the group. Shortly afterwards, we gave the group a norm referenced test on decimals and found that most scored above average for their age. Julia's reaction to the test had been, "That test you gave us yesterday was easy." We then explained that in fact many pupils found it more difficult than her. Some of her friends in higher Maths sets would now be slower and less accurate than she was. This test score now became a point of reference for herself and for us.

Having decided they could "do" decimals, Julia's group now went on to fractions. In many textbooks, decimals are seen as a kind of fraction and even though fractions are now used much less than decimals, it is assumed that children will master fractions more easily. Actually many find them more difficult. The sequence of numbers and the use of symbols can be particularly confusing. Julia knew that 0.5 was the same as one half, and that 1 pie chart cut into two pieces gave us ½. Having distributed calculators we asked the group to put in:

$$1 \div 2 =$$

The answer was of course 0.5. We then asked the group to spot the connection between the number ½ and the sequence 1 ÷ 2. At first they just saw that both were 0.5. Then they looked more closely at the symbols. The division sign was very similar to the horizontal bar in the fraction. Some of them with computers knew that the division sign on a micro had no dots /. So one half was the same as:

$$\frac{1}{2} = 1 / 2 = 1 \div 2 = 0.5$$

Similarly:

$$\frac{1}{10} = 1 / 10 = 1 \div 10 = 0.1$$

The group now began to realize the significance of the symbols and the sequence of numbers. They could be translated into a set of instructions which the calculator could then "read". As Martin said, "It's just like English."

For the textbook the next logical step was the addition and subtraction of fractions through conversion to decimals. For quite a few calculators this is the simplest of questions:

1/4 + 1/2 =

becomes:

1 ÷ 4 = (display shows 0.25) + 1 (display shows 1) ÷ 2 = 0.75

But other calculators produce quite different results:

1 ÷ 4 = (display shows 0.25) + 1 (display shows 1.25) ÷ 2 = 0.625

Unfortunately, Julia's group had the second kind of calculator. The calculator instructions advise one to multiply the second denominator by the first numerator:

2 x 1 ÷ 4 (display shows 0.5) + 1 (display shows 1.5) ÷ 2 = 0.75

Julia would not have understood the reason for this, nor would she have wanted to follow a meaningless ritual. To have attempted it might have undermined her faith in both the calculator and her own ability to "do" fractions. We simply got the group to convert the first fraction, write it down, convert the second fraction write that down, then add the first conversion:

1/4 = 0.25 (clear display) 1/2 = 0.5 + 0.25 = 0.75

Given the confusion that Julia and the rest of the group had previously felt about fractions, we felt this was as far as we wanted to take them this year. Normally so useful, the calculator could itself have generated extra difficulties. In the fourth year, however, the group learned how to add and subtract without conversion. We prepared the ground by looking at ratios and equivalence. They found by cross multiplying that 1/3 and 2/6 were equivalent:

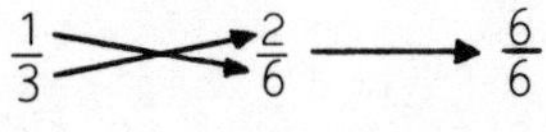

and then generated series of equivalent fractions:

1/3 = 2/6 = 3/9 = 4/12 = 5/15 = 10/30

1/4 = 2/8 = 3/12 = 4/16 = 5/20 = 10/40

They then used these for adding:

1/3 + 1/4 =
1/3 = 4/12 : 1/4 = 3/12
4/12 + 3/12 = 7/12

By now Julia's group was following a Mode III C.S.E. course. 50% of the marks had to be allotted to a final exam, but the other 50% were divided between a series of problem solving and mental arithmetic tests at termly intervals, a project and a number of mathematical topics. For the project the teacher offered the class a range of worksheets which offered the pupils some guidance in how to analyse the work in mathematical terms. Julia wanted to follow up something she was enjoying on her child care course about the nutritional needs of a toddler. The project was profusely illustrated with pictures of babies and babyfoods. There were articles on allergens and cholesterol, but the heart of it, from a mathematical point of view, was an analysis of what a cousin of hers had eaten during the course of a week, broken down into calories, vitamins, proteins etc.

One of the boys in the group whose father was a long distance lorry driver, and who was fascinated with trucking did a project about going on holiday to the South of Italy in the lorry. It was illustrated with maps and pictures from holiday brochures. Adrian worked out the distance, through measuring the map in mm, then finding the scale and doing the necessary calculations. His father told him the miles per gallon and he then converted that to Km per litre. Lastly he found the amount of petrol needed and so calculated the fuel costs of the journey.

One could argue that there is very little difference between these project lessons and the practical problems set by the Inner-City teacher described at the beginning of the chapter. The crucial point, however, is that the difficulties which children like Julia and Adrian might run into had been foreseen by their teacher. The skills they needed would have been thoroughly rehearsed in advance. And for these two pupils, there was something to work for.

A few schools get the whole of the bottom 20% to follow a Mode III C.S.E. course like this and then select those who have a reasonable chance of Grade 4 or above for entry. Others gather together a file of the pupils' tests, topics and projects and present them, together with a Maths reference, to the pupils. These can then be taken to 'job' interviews. Other teachers argue that employers are unimpressed by C.S.E. Mode III Grade 4's and pupil files. They prefer an R.S.A. Foundation Course or a C.S.E. Mode I arithmetic, more mechanical though they may be. One hopes that many of these issues will soon be resolved by the introduction of pupil profiles and G.C.S.E.

All too often, the attainments of the least able are of little interest to Maths Departments. One fears that many of the staff concerned will continue to reinforce the low expectations of the pupils and there will be little hope of establishing a consistent pattern of success. Maths will continue to be poorly assessed, narrowly conceived, mechanical and boring. Children with a history of learning difficulties will continue with little to aim for and little expected of them. Not only will people leave school with unnecessary large problems in the survival skills, the curiosity, insight and intelligence they do possess will have been wasted. Present initial training and in-service policies have to bear much of the responsibility for this.

REFERENCES

A.P.U. (1982) Third Secondary Mathematics Survey : HMSO
Cockcroft Report (1982) Mathematics Counts : HMSO
Holt, J. (1964) How Children Fail : Penguin

FURTHER READING

Ablewhite, R.C. (1969) Mathematics and the Less Able : Heinemann
Ainscow, M. and Tweddle, D.A. (1979) Preventing Classroom Failure : An Objectives Approach : Wiley
Brissenden, T.H.F. (1979) Teacher Pupil Discussion in Mathematics in Schools : 8:3 : 29-32
Dexter (1964) The Politics of Stupidity : in The Other Side : Ed Becker, H. : The Free Press
Duncan, A. (1978) Teaching Mathematics to Slow Learners : Ward Lock
Gal'piern, P. (1970) An Experimental Study in the Education of Mental Actions : in Readings in Educational Psychology : Ed Stones, E. : Methuen. See also extracts by Luria, Vigotsky and Kalingkova
Herndon, J. (1975) The Dumb Class:in Worlds Apart : Ed Beck : Collier MacMillan
Murray, J. (1981) Children's Understanding of Mathematics
Shuard, H. and Quadling, D. (1980) Teacher of Mathematics : Harper
Simmons, R. (1978) Colloquial Mathematics : in Mathematics in Schools : 7 : 6-7
Skemp, R.S. (1971) The Psychology of Learning Maths: Penguin

Chapter Six

THE WIDER CURRICULUM

One of the most urgent challenges of teacher education is to enable the whole range of mainstream staff to explore the contribution that they and their subjects can make to the curriculum of children with Special Needs. For most of such children there is no question of an entirely separate curriculum, taught by specialist teachers. A proportion of them will follow a modified curriculum; specialist teachers will continue to teach the basic skills and to offer their support in mainstream classes, but the subject departments of ordinary Secondary Schools are taking increasing responsibilities for their education.

One way of preparing teachers for this is for them to work in Special Needs Departments before and during teaching practice. In my own T.P. School we were encouraged to observe the work of all the staff, not just in our own specialities. My own experience in the Special Needs Department made me particularly interested in the staff whom these pupils thought were good. One was a Scientist. I wanted to ask him what he thought was the point in teaching science to the least able. Like many of the schools in the most deprived Inner-City areas, this had daily truancy rates of over 30% and over a third of the pupils were thought to reach the school leaving age functionally illiterate. Observing his lesson made me understand why the pupils enjoyed his lessons. Firstly he treated them with respect. He used words they could understand and got them to discuss their ideas with him in demonstrations. He let his class wander round the room in practicals, talking to each other. There was reading material and writing for the class, but it was suited to the children's capabilities. Above all he seemed committed to his subject. He wanted to communicate it to all children.

Later, a student on teaching practice in a very different school, who had been doing some work in a Special Needs Department to complement her specialist work in science, summed up the relationship between the two. She had been given a bottom set second year group. The homework she had set them was a disaster. Less than half the class had handed their books in. Several of those who had done the work had made little effort and even those who had tried had misunderstood the point of the lesson. She had felt very depressed about this, until she realized that some of the children she had been teaching in the Special Needs Department were in this bottom set. There were others, also, who had difficulties with the subject, even though their reading and writing were better.

This realization made her look at her work in a different light. Before, she had seen herself first and foremost as a teacher of science. She expected to have to teach her subject to the whole ability range, including children with Special Educational Needs. Now she also began to see her work as a contribution to the overall education of children with Special Needs. There had to be more of an overlap between the assessment she had been making of the children's skills in reading, writing and maths, through her work in the Special Needs Department, and the demands she could make on them through her science lessons. That is not to say that the children's reading and writing came first and that science is peripheral. Science has a body of knowledge and a set of skills to which all children should be entitled, but the way she explained a homework, used textbooks or helped her pupils write would need to reflect what she had learned in the Special Needs Department.

This student, Val, saw a subject specialist not as working in isolation, but as playing a part in the overall curriculum of the children she taught. When these children had Special Needs, the demands of the subject teacher should take into account and reinforce their abilities in the basic subjects. A competent science teacher should develop her pupils' reading, talking, measuring skills and so on. But Val also thought that in the particular case of her subject, there were other links between science and the fostering of reading skills. Science could be thought of as a process of identifying "relationships and patterns and trying to explain them". (D.E.S. 1985). There were particular insights only her subject could offer that enable us to make sense of the world. For children whose experience of school so often undermined a sense of meaning, these "explanations" were particularly important.

This sense of the interconnection of the comprehension elements of reading and the heuristic aspects of science could be clarified if we refer to Trevor, the fifteen year old with a reading age of eight, whose reading we looked at in the second chapter. Like many other children with considerable difficulties in the basic subjects, he was fascinated by science, its inventions and its explanations.

Despite his reading problems he obviously had a lively mind and when we asked him to choose a book to read, he said he was interested in the history of flight. The first chapter of the book we used was about the history of air balloons. As it happened he had just been doing "pressure" in his general science course, so he knew about the way hot air would make a balloon rise. Trevor used his knowledge of physics to help him get the gist of what he was reading. This understanding of what the passage was about in turn helped circumvent some of the decoding problems he was having. Strangely enough he could read some of the technical jargon more easily than shorter everyday words. We talked about the book, the scientific principles behind hot air balloons and his enjoyment of science. The fact that he could read this book, particularly the scientific words, prompted him to take it home and produce some science homework. He had copied out the story of the Montgolfier brothers and their original invention. But he had also replicated one of their early experiments, filling a paper bag full of hot air over his coal fire and watching it rise up the chimney. He then set about making a model balloon with a polythene bage and a small basket slung beneath, but when he had put that on the fire, it had burned up.

When I showed Trevor's written homework to his science teacher and told him it was one of Trevor's favourite lessons, he was puzzled. How could it be that a lad who could hardly copy off the blackboard, who never answered in class and who played the fool through his lessons, could actually say he was interested in pressure? Trevor seemed confused about so many of the things school offered him. What was there about science that fascinated him? In this particular instance, it was the discovery that he could read this book and the scientific words in it, his understanding of and identification with the story of the original inventors, and also his appreciation of a highly abstract and concise scientific explanation. Scientific concepts have a fascination which extends far beyond the top streams and 'O' level groups. Even amongst the children with Special Needs there is a capacity to understand relationships and patterns, to find the words that will express them and to test out their own explanations through experiment.

Doing this on a regular basis with bottom set groups or with children who are disaffected and difficult demands the highest skills of the teacher. One of the Biology teachers who allowed me to do some cooperative teaching had the knack. He was a very flexible, open minded teacher who allowed a great deal of pupil-pupil talk during practicals and who encouraged pupils' questions. Although he had a clear idea of what he wanted to get through in a lesson, he was good at picking up apparently stray pupil remarks which showed that they understood the scientific concepts behind the experiment. This came out particularly strikingly during a lesson on yeast. The class were given live and dead yeast, sugar, cold and hot water, boiling tubes and balloons. They were told to mix the substances in the boiling tubes in a certain order, then fit the balloons over the top of the glass tubes. Most of the pupils simply did as they were told and when the balloon swelled over one of the boiling tubes, it was of no great moment to them.

Mixed in with the poor readers, there were other children who found science difficult or who were poorly motivated or just plain difficult. One of these was a boy called David, who openly said he saw no point in school, apart from having a "laugh" and "mucking about" with his friends. He tried to turn all his lessons into a joke and he now made the remark that one of the test tubes was "breathing."

> "What do you mean breathing? If it is, it's only breathing out," said one of his mates.
>
> "How come?" said the teacher. "Is the yeast in this boiling tube alive or dead?"
>
> "It's alive," said David.

"When you're alive, do you just breathe out?"

"No you breathe in as well," said someone else from across the class.

"You breathe in oxygen," said another.

"And who can remember what you breathe out?" said the teacher.

"Carbon Dioxide."

"So what's funny about live yeast?"

"It breathes out but it does not breathe in"

"And what does it breathe out?"

"Carbon Dioxide," said another pupil.

"How do you know?" asked the teacher.

"Yeah, how do you know?" asked David.

"Let's find out."

It's rare for a class to cover so much ground so quickly. Often this process runs out of steam, there are false leads and teachers have to interrupt the discussion to discipline someone. It is particularly demanding having to listen to pupil chatter and pick out the interesting comments, if one has reason to be worried about controlling pupils and if the pupils are wandering round a lab., using expensive and breakable equipment. The pupil's language will often be at odds with scientific jargon, too, and the teacher has difficulty explicating the concepts in words the children will understand. Even this teacher frequently hesitated in the course of a question and answer session before he found a word or a phrase that conveyed the meaning of a scientific concept, but yet was readily accessible to children whose vocabulary was limited and listening skills poor.

In this instance the teacher had been trying to communicate the concept of anaerobic respiration. David's use of the word "breathing", and his friend's reply that "It's only breathing out" were sufficiently close to the meaning of anaerobic respiration for him to want to seize on that phrase.

There was more to this incident than the teacher's successful use of pupil language, though. The teacher was also using a discovery to teach about the scientific process. David had wanted to have a laugh at the expense of the lesson. What he had inadvertantly done was show that there was something "funny" about live yeast. Normally, if you put chemicals in a test tube, they react but they are still inanimate. But if you put hot water and sugar with the live yeast, they come alive and start to "breathe".

It may be that much of the talk that goes on round practicals is inarticulate or irrelevant. For pupils in low ability science groups, who might well think of themselves as "thick" or failures or bad, the moment of cognitive dissonance, where what they see conflicts with what they believe, can well be experienced as "a laugh." The child who spots the incongruity between inert chemicals and living things, living things that breathe oxygen and living things that do not, may well be the child with the highest IQ, or the poorest reader or the most difficult in the class. As a cooperative teacher, one could observe these conversations, reformulate the basic ideas for the pupils with writing difficulties, get them to rehearse their own explanations and use these as the basis for their written work. One wanted all the children to take part in the process of scientific thinking. Wherever teachers can manage pupil talk in such a way that all the class feel they have an opportunity to contribute their ideas, science becomes more relevant and a means of overcoming low expectations.

It might be objected that we are not attempting to train children with Special Needs to become research scientists and that, with a large syllabus to get through, there is not enough time for pupils to think it out for themselves. Yet if pupils feel that they are merely taking on teachers' ideas, they miss an opportunity to generate their own explanations, to internalise them and to put them in their own words. They forget that scientists are people like themselves and that science is a man-made set of ideas. Without this sense of a common pursuit, science degenerates into alchemy, a set of immutable beliefs which are unamenable to reason or experience. Despite the fact that they cannot read, that they don't always speak the teacher's language and that they find many of their lessons boring and difficult, quite a few children with Special Needs can be encouraged to enjoy spotting the apparent unreasonableness of the universe and resolving their own doubts through question, answer and practical work.

Many of these points could also be made about the teaching of Humanities subjects to children with Special Needs, even though each has its distinctive bodies of knowledge, skills and experiences. It is unfortunately the case that religion is often taught as if it were only a body of knowledge and that it is perceived by pupils to have little relevance. While they teach pupils about Christianity and the world religion, too many teachers evade the experiences that make religion a common pursuit for different people. One of the teachers who seemed to have resolved this problem and generated an intelligent interest in R.E. amongst children with Special Needs was a student with a degree in comparative religion, who said she found the way people expressed their own ideas about religion one of the most fascinating things she knew.

It is extremely difficult to encourage pupils to explore religious experiences and symbols without turning the subject into a process of induction. But if we can build on the pupils' own ideas and experiences, the subject can be extraordinarily satisfying. The issues that emerge and the arguments that arise have a peculiar force and significance. In one second year mixed ability class, materials and books had been given out for small-group project work on the creation myths. We had started with Adam and Eve. There were clear sets of objectives for the lesson, both in terms of the knowledge to be gained and the skills to be used. Some of the most able were to take notes from a range of sources and then write their own account. The least able were given structured questions on a single text, whose answers could then be turned into continuous prose. One group's work was being held up by a child who said, "I don't believe in God, anyway." His atheism was so strongly felt, it challenged the whole point of the lesson. It seemed an ideal opportunity to ask the rest of the class what they really felt about God and creation." What do we mean by God? Do we think there is any part of us that God created? Is there anything in us or in the world that we think of as God-like?"

At first it was as if the class did not know what to make of the questions. They wanted to have them repeated. Gradually the answers came in. From some of the children one heard "Jesus is God" or "God is love." Some replied with conviction, others as if they expected teacher to tell them that this was the correct answer. One group of children clearly thought that God was in their conscience. They knew the difference between right and wrong without needing to be told. The knowledge seemed to come from the deepest part of them.

Jimmy, a difficult boy and one of the backward readers, responded quite differently. He took on what the other pupils were saying about the deepest part of themselves, but his life's experience had made him interpret this another way. And he used metaphors and symbols of his own. He said that the deepest part of him was fear. The effect on the class was extraordinary. Jimmy was one of the biggest lads in the second year and he was a bully. Yet he was revealing that underneath all this, he was afraid. He went on:

> "When I was about ten I had this dream I was Captain Marvel. I leapt out of bed in my Captain Marvel clothes and I knew I did not have to be afraid any more. So now Captain Marvel is a kind of God to me."

The account of Jimmy's dream fascinated the class. In a way, it was even more challenging than the other child's assertion that he did not believe in God. It also set off a kind of cognitive dissonance in the pupils. On the one hand they had been arguing about Christian ideas. On the other here was Jimmy talking about another completely different idea, which he was convinced was true. They did not have to believe that Captain Marvel was a kind of God for them. They couldn't tell Jimmy his ideas were wrong either. What they wanted was an intellectual apparatus that would allow them to take both of these sets of ideas into account.

One had to refer them back to their study of religion and show them that for all of us, young and old, rich and poor, prehistoric and modern, there are anxieties about identity, the meaning of life and death which we can only approach through symbols and parables. The words "Panic", "Titanic" and "Olympic" were put on the board. All of them were known to the class, and they saw that they were connected because of the "ic" at the end. It was explained that all three were Greek words, that they were thousands of years old and they all related to the experiences Jimmy was telling us about through his dream. The Ancient Greeks called their God of nature Pan. If one wandered in the woods and got lost, one would feel overwhelmed by nature and "panic". I told them about the Titans and their superhuman strength, but how Zeus and the Gods from Mount Olympus tricked them with their greater cunning and destroyed them. For the Jews and the Christians there was a very different account of the creation and of the relationship between aspects of God. Adam and Eve experienced fear and rejection - perhaps their expulsion from Eden had even filled them with Panic. But for Jews and Christians this rejection was seen as Mankind's responsibility.

The difference between Captain Marvel and the Biblical Creator was explored. All of us knew what Jimmy was talking about and that neither Fear nor Power could be easily dismissed. Going back to the original assertion of atheism, we could see that the statement that we do not believe in God is not as simple as it appears. Jimmy's dream had shown that while we do not all believe in The God of the Bible, there are experiences which have a huge symbolic effect on us. Whatever we feel to be deepest in us affects our sense of identity and our beliefs about the world. Captain Marvel could be said to have shaped a part of Jimmy's identity. Our Gods might be that kind of fearlessness, or love, or money or the conscience that tells us we have responsibility for our actions. Jimmy himself was one of the most challenging and tragic children I have ever taught and he ended up unemployed, homeless and destitute.

Myths and legends can communicate themselves across the boundaries of class, culture and ability. This became clear in my probationary year. We had a supply teacher called Robert Lagnardo who was specifically employed by the ILEA to be a story teller. For someone who was teaching Humanities to classes of the most deprived Inner-City children his lessons were a revelation. He did not impose silence on them, they seemed to hang on his every word. He would enter into role, often fleetingly and subtly, and allow the pupils to see the situation from each of the characters' viewpoints. He used the simplest language with considerable force and expressiveness. And he made sure the pupils saw the point of a story. One of the most effective he told my class was about the nineteenth century Zulu Chief, Shaka. Half my first years were first or second generation emigrants from the Caribbean and they normally reacted with deep suspicion to any material about Africa.

As we have seen, the ability to comprehend and use narrative structure seems to precede children's grasp of non-fictional accounts. It can play a crucial part in the way Secondary children with Special Needs develop a sense of coherence in their written work. In many Humanities courses one is asked to follow a syllabus which is built upon analytical ideas. The objectives of a term's work in History may include an understanding of ther development of Canals or of Iron smelting. Yet it can all seem remote and abstract, nothing to do with real people, irrelevant and boring. For classes which include numbers of children with Special Needs, narrative can provide a means of generating empathy with those who made the past - not only the great Iron-masters and Canal builders, but the ordinary navvies and labourers. It can also help one explore the viewpoints of those whose culture is not only different but occasionally antipathetic to the pupils'. Before the story-teller came, I was having great difficulty finding a way of teaching Eighteenth Century British History to a mixed ability third year group. The textbook was too difficult for the poor readers, some topics seemed too dry and abstract, and others were frankly divisive. The expansion of the British Empire and the development of the Slave Trade meant that for half of my class, the eighteenth century was a time of progress and of the gratification of national pride. For the forebears of the other half, this period had meant shame, exploitation and mass murder.

One way of linking all these topics and providing a conceptual framework which would allow all the pupils from the least to the most able to see a pattern in these events was to produce a long running historical novel. We started with the agricultural revolution and the story of an East Anglian couple on "Turnip" Townsend's estate. Though they had not wanted to introduce the agricultural improvements that were asked of them, the winter feeding of cattle meant there was more food for their children. This helped one of them survive an attack of smallpox. The next episode was about one of their sons who took the surplus vegetables to market in London, and then stayed on to work in one of the new factories. This allowed us to look at the Industrial Revolution. The average and able children could read about this in the textbooks and in the project collection we borrowed from the Library. The third instalment was about a grandson who started life as a chimney sweep, but who ran away to sea to become involved in the Slave Trade. Just as the English adolescent was preparing for life at sea, we broke off and introduced another family from West Africa. The fourth chapter was about how one of their adolescent children had been captured and enslaved by another African tribe during a local war and then sold to the British agent on the coast. Having survived incarceration at the British fort, he was then put on board the white boy's ship for the fifth episode: the journey to Jamaica. In the epidemics that swept the ship, the boys' destinies were linked. They both fell ill and both recovered, their spirits unbroken. Soon after they reached the Caribbean both boys tried to run away. The sixth part described how the African was sent to a sugar plantation, then ran away to join the remnants of Cudjoe's rebels in the hills. The seventh showed the English boy back in England, sickened by conditions in the Slave Trade and attempting to jump ship. But he was then impressed by the Royal Navy, to play his part in the Napoleonic War.

The writing of this historical novel made one feel one was learning the language that pupils used. It allowed one to relate the body of knowledge in our history syllabus more closely to the empathetic aspects of history teaching. And it made one re-examine political events and social changes from the viewpoint of ordinary people the same age or only a little older than these third years. At a technical level, there was a perpetual problem of bringing in historical detail, without submerging the sense of narrative. Where the class textbook or the library collections provided relevant pictures these were referred to in the questions at the end of each chapter, so the story itself provided a stepping stone to the pupils' use of resource material. We drew family trees as we went along, and then a series of time charts. There were columns for the main events in the English and West African family lives, for the main inventions in agriculture and industry and for domestic political and imperial history.

With other groups who did not have the same degree of deprivation and for whom it seemed more possible to teach higher order historical skills, this very heavy reliance on a narrative structure seemed an encumbrance. The empathetic involvement one wanted could be achieved through a range of techniques. This variety could then allow one to focus on skills like note taking and the use of notes in continuous writing. With another second year mixed ability class, we wanted to get across the idea of the relationship between the agricultural revolution and migration to the cities. We also thought that all the class, even those with a history of learning difficulties, could write something about this. The ground had been thoroughly prepared with lessons on the actual inventions, the impact of enclosures and the growth of the urban population. We brought all this together with a piece of improvised drama. Some children wanted speaking parts and these were given the roles of bailiff, the dispossessed family and their urban neighbours. Those who were more shy were lined up in rows at the front of the class and asked to act as the moving parts in one of the new mills. The climax of the story came when one of the pupils, playing the part of a small boy, got caught in the "machine". In the next lesson, the average and able pupils who could write an objective account were shown how to structure an essay.

The first paragraph was on changes in the countryside, the second on migration to the cities and the last on the way this generated extra "hands" for the new industries. Those with a history of learning difficulties wrote a story about the migration from the little boy's point of view, using a similar sequence of paragraphs.

Other people's fiction could be used. For average and able children studying the inter-war years, research on the prose of the period could be included in the objectives: for those with reading difficulties one could read out passages from "Love on the Dole" or "Borstal Boy". This can lead on to a lesson in the construction of notes. The pupils compile a list of questions and the teacher plays the role of a fictional character to answer them. Questions and answers are put up on the board in a random order as pupils come up with them. The teacher then shows how one idea naturally leads on to another and links these notes with arrows, as in a Buzan diagram.

Having got their pupils to practice mock interviews in school, some teachers then take along tape recorders on outside visits. With one group of children on a visit to a Roman Road, the History teacher played the part of the Centurion who supervised its building. We discovered that this stretch of roadway was not absolutely straight, as the textbook suggested. We formed the pupils into lines and found that there was just enough room for ten heavily laden children to march abreast. Information about when the road was built and why, how it fed into the system of Roman Roads in Britain was given by the "Centurion". The tape was then played back to the class in school. The Buzan diagram was constructed from the recorded comments and questions. We then re-analysed it creating subsections on dates, purposes, building specifications and construction. And with the memory of the visit still fresh in their minds, and a set of notes which helped them organize their ideas, even the slow learners in the class saw how they could write an essay.

Rather than use the historical essay as a model of continuous prose, many teachers pick on an event, produce the note diagrams and then analyse them as a newspaper editor would. Getting the children to pick out the note that could be used as the main headline, helps them to distinguish how significant facts are. The key concept is stencilled across the top of the article in letters two inches high. The next most important ideas are subheadings and the rest of the material is put into the linking paragraphs. The critical moment in the event is made the subject of a picture or cartoon. The finished article can be displayed in the classroom on colourful backing paper, so that the work looks attractive.

Some apparently difficult pupils and slow learners readily learn the skills of interviewing. Their history teacher may then feel confident enough to let them visit Day Centres and talk to old people about what life was like when they were young. For some children with Special Needs this not only encourages the interest in historical research, it also develops and extends the core skills of talking and listening, reading, writing and Maths.

One mixed ability first year group working on an interdisciplinary Village Survey, found an old man who had spent all his life working in the village shop. As well as helping them to make a survey of contemporary prices, he told them how expensive some articles were when he started work in the 1920's. We took their tape back to school and showed the two girls who had done the interview how to work out the amount that prices had gone up. They got so interested in this, they borrowed part of the local history collection the library had lent us and started their own project on the village. Night after night they worked away, copying a great deal to start with, then learning to skim and precis. They ended up filling two notebooks in a fortnight, teaching themselves far more about reading and writing through this Humanities project than they were learning in English. One of these girls eventually achieved an 'O' level in English Language, something that very occasionally happens to children who start their Secondary careers with reading difficulties, and it may well have been that success in this project helped her overcome low expectations.

Many of these approaches can be used in Geography, as a way of heightening children's interest in the body of knowledge and of making its specific skills easier to acquire. In a set of lessons on the Australian semi-desert with one second year Special Needs group, we started by telling the story of "Walkabout", reading parts of the easy read version and discussing what it would be like to be stranded there. Next we read a factual account and looked at pictures from the textbook. The class were introduced to note taking by being asked to remember as many points as they could from this account. These were written up on the blackboard, then grouped under various headings: climate, how climate affects what grows, how vegetation affects man and so on. Lastly everything is rubbed off the board except the headings and the class has then to make its own notes under each of the headings.

Where Geography departments have extensive resource collections, these can make the job of teaching Special Needs groups easier. Reading a textbook account of the Australian mining industry can be made more vivid if ore samples are then distributed. The first time I tried this, I failed to label or number the specimens and I let the class have all ten of them at the same time. It was quite impossible to keep track of them and only nine were returned. A good idea went wrong and I had a disciplinary problem on my hands. Again, if one wants to make a model with children who are not used to practical work in Humanities lessons, one has to think out one's approach carefully and anticipate the problems one might run into. In a lesson about artesian basins, we made a grand start by lining a work tray with a sheet of polythene and a layer of plasticine. These represented the impervious rocks and we showed how well they held the water. We then put some sand in a test tube and showed that if you put water on top of it, it seeped down. We made a well out of an empty biro tube, then covered the plasticine with a layer of sand. We poured water onto one side of the tray and waited for it to seep across. Unfortunately the water took much longer to seep under the "desert" than we had anticipated. We poured on more and more water, but none reached our well. The children began to lose interest. It was as if they stopped thinking that this experiment was proper work and started to see it as an opportunity to "muck about" with sand and water. We had to stop that part of the lesson before trouble started. Two weeks later, however, we used the same materials to make a model of the Snowy Mountains Scheme. This time we showed that even though "rain" only fell one side of the mountains, a pipeline could make the land on the other side fruitful. This lesson was a great success.

Many children with Special Needs have great difficulty reading and drawing maps. Even something as fundamental as locating London on a map of the U.K. can be thoroughly confusing. Children who have difficulty decoding sets of letters find it hard to distinguish between the symbols on a map. And many of the concepts map makers employ, like direction, scale and contours relate to mathematical concepts which children with learning difficulties may never have been taught. A few teachers would argue that the teaching of complex skills like these is ideally suited to behavioural analysis.

Those using this approach would start by asking what subskills the pupils need in order to demonstrate competence. In a first year mixed ability class studying the Ordance Survey 3 figure grid reference system, one would find children who will be able to give the coordinates of a certain village or railway station after minimal instruction. But there will also be children who are completely lost. One would first want to find out what aspects of the task were causing the problems. Some might find the basic figure-ground configuration confusing. They might not realise that a point on a grid also refers to a symbol on the map. Others might find it hard to differentiate left/right and up/down, whilst another group might not be able to follow the sequence: left to right; then down to up.

Having diagnosed those aspects of the task that are causing difficulties to the pupils, we then devised precise step by step tasks. The tasks are constructed in such a way that competence is testable at each stage. For pupils with these fairly extreme problems, one may start with a simple worksheet set out in a chessboard pattern. The bottom line of squares are labelled A-H, the left hand side 1-8, from bottom to top. The children are then asked to draw the outline of a Treasure Map on this pattern. They might want to make it into an island, or add rivers and mountains, but in one square they must have a buried treasure and in another a man-trap. The group with extreme problems may then be split into pairs and they play a version of "Battleships". Some pupils might very quickly show they have grasped the connection between the coordinates and the location of a point on a map and that they can use the 'x' and 'y' coordinates correctly. For other pupils with continuing problems, one then has to find other tasks which will keep up the children's motivation. Some schools keep versions of these games on computer discs. Finding the treasure makes the computer play a victory tune and produce some colourful graphics.

For the next stage, the easily distinguishable letter/number code is dropped and numbers only are employed. The chessboard pattern may now have a series of simple symbols on it, circles, triangles and crosses. Criteria of competence are assessed. A pupil who consistently finds the coordinates of 8 out of 10 symbols will be judged to have achieved mastery of this stage. For pupils who score less and are losing motivation, further games would have to be devised.

For the third stage, pupils are given small pieces of graph paper with a few Ordnance Survey Symbols on them: church, battlefield and station. Each of the larger squares along the 'x' and 'y' axes are numbered 0, 1, 2, 3, but the pupils have to number the smaller squares in between themselves. They then have to locate the symbols using two figure grid reference notation. When they can score 8 out of 10 or more correct on this kind of exercise, the pupils are given graph paper squares labelled with two-figure numbers and shown how to use the Ordnance Survey System. More and more of their symbols are employed. And the last stage involves the use of an actual map. Pupil success is carefully monitored at each stage and if any task seems not to be working very successfully, it can be changed. At its best, the use of behavioural objectives allows the teacher continuous feedback in how to improve his own approaches.

Behavioural analysis is an area of controversy in Special Education. There are teachers who would suggest that it discounts the experience pupils themselves bring to a subject and that it rules out both the subjective and the spontaneous aspects of the learning process. Too narrow a preoccupation with intended outcomes may blind the teacher to unintended consequences. Too precise a differentiation of learning tasks for a mixed ability group may undermine the self-esteem and motivation of the very pupils one was trying to help. To a certain extent, the argument has moved on from curriculum development to curriculum evaluation and it is of limited interest to serving teachers. In a practical situation, projects that involve children across the ability range can often be structured so that subskills are taught in sequence through precise tasks but the work given those with learning difficulties can be related to their experiences and be made to appear high status to the rest of the group.

Another of the concepts associated with map-reading which causes problems is the interpretation of contours. Many pupils find it difficult to grasp that one can represent a hill with lines on a two dimensional diagram, or that these lines are used to "map" points which are all the same height above sea-level, perhaps because they also find it hard to follow a given contour line or to distinguish a set of lines which are too close together or which wander too far apart. A way round this is to introduce the concept, when the syllabus demands it, then return to a more in-depth study after the class have been on a visit to a place where there are hills or mountains - expedition day, a school trip or a specially arranged Geography visit. There will be a shared experience on which to draw. The class will remember that the ground was level on a certain part of a walk, that in a certain place they were overlooked by high ground and in another, a stream flowed downhill past them. One then produces maps of the area and shows the class where the land was steep and flat. One asks the pupils what they notice about the contour lines in these places.

For those who experience difficulties with the differentiation of a set of lines, a simplified worksheet contour map of one part of the area can be brought in. Groups of pupils then trace one contour each. Then tracing paper shapes can be cut out and transposed onto thick cardboard. The cardboard shapes are then stuck together and the pupils learn from experience that lines on a map can make a three dimensional model of a place they visited. The Biology teacher mentioned earlier in this chapter was also a keen Geologist. When he did this kind of exercise with children who found the concept of contours difficult, he got them to smooth out the cardboard steps in the model using "tetrion". The whole hillside was then painted, model trees put on, river courses, roads and footpaths indicated. He had ambitious plans to take bottom set school leavers on an expedition to a local valley with a history of Iron Ore production, show them the rudiments of height surveying and then build a vast model of the area, complete with abandoned railways. This could then be displayed on Parents Evenings.

This kind of project approach still contains within it an element of diagnosis. The tasks set the class are differentiated and the skills they teach are clearly testable. The simplified worksheet contour map could easily lead on to more sophisticated kinds. But for the teacher and the pupils the aim is the production of a piece of work which is seen to be worthwhile in its own terms. And it leads on to a seemingly deeper - if undemonstrable - imaginative awareness of the spatial concepts Geographers and Mathematicians share.

The curricular area that causes greatest concern to those responsible for children with Special Needs at the moment is the teaching of Modern Languages. It is often said that children who have difficulties in reading and writing their own language will be only be confused by another. Many schools withdraw children from French for extra English. Others allow Special Needs groups to follow a course for just one year. All too often, lessons consist of a short grammatical exercise followed by drawing, colouring in and labelling. The points covered present too remote and analytical a view of language. One probationary French teacher called James described a particularly sterile exercise he had had to teach a bottom set second year class. It was on the use of "de" after a negative, instead of "de la" or "du". The children had been very restless and James thought that this was because the lesson had so little to do with their experience of language. Very few of them seemed to appreciate the logical distinction between "some" and "any", in English. They could use them easily enough, as in the sentences:

I have some apples
I haven't any apples

and they also knew that:

I haven't some apples

was wrong. However, they were just as likely to say:

I haven't no apples

as

I haven't any apples

Their view of what was correct and incorrect did not seem to come from a logical analysis of language rules, rather from what "sounded O.K" and from what "everybody else says." They would not use "I haven't some apples" because nobody would understand what they meant. This was not to argue that pupils with learning difficulties should not do his subject. James just felt that the objectives of his syllabus and its view of "correct speech" were dubious.

James himself felt that his aim should be getting the pupils to make themselves understood. He thought that we should start with the notion of survival skills. Just as one's aim for those who had the greatest difficulty with reading should be to enable them to read signs like exit, pay here, ladies and gentlemen, and for the very weakest mathematician to make change, tell the time and measure, so there must be certain language situations, mastery of which would help one to survive abroad. The language generated could be built up into a graded course. The starting point would have to be talking and listening, and reading and writing would have to be based on spoken interaction. James wanted to develop role play situations where pupils could practise making themselves understood.

There is a distinct lack of interest in Modern Languages among those concerned with Curriculum Development in Special Education. Publications as central as Brennan's "The Curricular Needs of Slow Learners" do not even mention French. Perhaps in the future, linguists will develop courses which enable children with difficulties in their own language to communicate more easily in another. Until then one feels that there are practical and theoretical problems for which those who are starting to teach are as likely to find answers as traditional remedial and special school staff, subject specialists or psychologists. There is still considerable freedom to experiment and innovate. And it may be that reflecting on what happens as one teaches one's subject to children with Special Needs becomes the most fruitful way of learning about both pupils and curriculum.

In many schools, Special Needs staff are spending less time taking their own classes and more going into those of subject specialists on a cooperative basis. This can be rather uncomfortable for any teacher at first and many prefer to cope in their own. It can be quite difficult learning to share a class, particularly to share the discipline. Each of us has his own limits of tolerance,and though all teachers find certain pupils difficult and though we all find that teaching brings out the worst in us from time to time, we do not want to be observed at these moments. Even so, cooperative teaching can enable one to reflect on these kinds of curricular issues much more deeply and to relate them to the day to day practice of teaching.

It may be that the Special Needs staff appear to do very little in one's first lessons with them. Their interventions will probably start with them quietly joining a small group of pupils as they get on with their writing or practical work. Sometimes the group they focus on will be mainly comprised of those with Special Needs, but this will not always be so. When the cooperative teacher and specialist have begun to get used to each others' approach, they might want to define more exactly who is responsible for which aspect of the lesson. One might be putting across the body of knowledge, whilst the other is helping with the skills. These skills might be subject specific ones like map making or the language skills that run across the curriculum.

Some pupils will know how to skim and precis and they can be encouraged to add ideas of their own or facts they have picked up elsewhere. At the other extreme pupils who find the textbook difficult to read may need help with this and, afterwards, they can be given a few oral comprehension questions to point out the main points.

If one is solely responsible for a class, it is often difficult to divide one's time satisfactorily between maintaining order and checking individuals' understanding. A lesson or so a week of cooperative teaching with a Special Needs teacher can be a valuable adjunct to teaching in a Special Needs Department. One is again brought into much closer contact with the pupils, one can assess their needs as they relate to a particular subject area and one can discuss them with someone who has this larger cross-curricular perspective. And as an additional advantage, though many classroom confrontations are defused by having two teachers in a classroom, cooperative teaching can also help one to look with more detachment at how one deals with difficult pupils.

REFERENCES

Behan, B. (1958) Borstal Boy: Hutchinson
Brennan, W.K. (1979) Curricular Needs of Slow Learners: Evans Methuen
Buzan, T. (1974) Use Your Head : BBC Publications
Greenwood, W. (1933) Love on the Dole : Cape

FURTHER READING

Ainslow, H. and Tweddle, D.A. (1979) Preventing Classroom failure : An Objective Approach : Wiley
Atkinson, P. and Delamont, S. (1977) Mock ups and Cock ups : The Stage Management of Guided Discovery Instruction : in School Experience : Ed Woods, P. and Hammersley, M. : Croom Helm
Barnes, D. et al (1971) Language, the Learner and the School : Penguin
Boardman, D. (1982) Geography with Slow Learners : Geographical Association
Burns, M.A. (1984) Differentiation and Cooperative Teaching : Modern Languages in Scotland : 26 : 71-80
Coltham, J.B. and Fines, J. (1971) Educational Objectives for the Study of History : Historical Association
D.E.S. (1985) The Curriculum From 5 to 16 : HMSO
D.E.S. (1983) The School Curriculum : HMSO
Geographical Assosiation. (1982) Teaching Geography to Less Able 11-14 year olds
Hull, J. (1980) Practical Points in Teaching History to Less Able Secondary Pupils : in Teaching History : 28 : 14-23
Keddie, N. (1971) Classroom Knowledge : in New Directions for the Sociology of Knowledge : Ed Young, M.F.D. : Collier MacMillan
Lunzer, E.A. and Gardner, K. Eds (1981) Reading for Learning in the Secondary School : Unpublished c Schools Council
McIver, V. (1982) Teaching History to Slow Learning Children in Secondary Schools: Stranmills' College Belfast
Pick, W. and Renwick, M. (1984) Teaching the Less Able Student in Geography : in The Geography Teachers' Guide to the Classroom : Ed Fien, J. et al : MacMillan
Rogers, P.J. (1980) The New History : The Historical Association

Sutton, C.R. (1979) Language and Communication in Science Lessons : in The Art of the Science Teacher Ed Sutton, C.R. and Hayson, J.T. : Science Teacher Education Project : McGraw Hill

Vulliamy, G. (1975) What Counts as School Music : in Explorations in the Politics of School Knowledge : Ed Whitty, G. and Young, M.F.D. : Nafferton Books

Whitty, G. (1977) Experiencing School Knowledge : The Case of Social Studies : in School Experience : Ed Woods, P. and Hammersley, M. : Croom Helm

Chapter Seven

DIFFICULT CHILDREN

On the visit made during my own P.G.C.E. course to an Inner-City Comprehensive School, described earlier in the chapter on Maths, we had coffee with the Deputy Head Pastoral. He lectured us about the lack of preparedness of student teachers. There were no lectures these days about keeping control. All the emphasis had passed to Curriculum and Psychology. In his opinion, the first lesson we should learn was how to become aware of what was happening in the classroom, so as to forestall trouble before it started. One of our group, David, asked the Deputy Head whether this was not too custodial a view of teaching. The Deputy said that David was free to try out his ideas there and then. He was just about to take the most difficult class in the school: the Easter leavers. David could teach them for him and the rest of us could watch.

So without any more time to prepare a lesson, we were led through the school to a class full of sullen fifteen year olds. The Deputy made them stand up and sit down and then he formally introduced them to us student teachers. He told them that we would be in charge for the rest of the morning and then he left. David's teaching style was quite different from that of the Deputy. He spoke easily and naturally as if he expected the class to reply. He said that he was on a visit to their school and that he would like them to tell him what being in this school was really like.

One sensed that this was enough to throw these boys off balance. They were not sure how to respond. Here was an adult who had taken charge of the situation with some determination but yet was deliberately relaxed and vulnerable. Slowly the class began to open up, describing the boredom of their lessons, the sense that they were cut off from many of the worthwhile things the school had to offer. They had no responsibilities and they were bossed about by Fifth Years who were Prefects and who tried to treat them like kids. They could not take exams either, and without qualifications they felt it was hardly worthwhile coming to school. They hated being shown up - by prefects or staff who thought they were "hard". They also hated the teachers who tried to be "hard", but who were too "soft" to follow through their orders and threats.

Gradually the sullenness eased, and one felt that these "difficult" children were being direct, thoughtful and honest. Through the kind of leadership he was offering, David had got them to be much more open and reflective. When he asked them what kinds of teachers they liked, they were positive, too. Good teachers were strict when they had to be, but not all the time. You could have a laugh with them, too. And they gave them interesting things to do. The Deputy Head kept peering round the door from time to time, but he did not intervene.

David's lesson made an extraordinary impression on us P.G.C.E. students. Children labelled as the most difficult in the school had become amenable and responsive. The Deputy Head had warned us that some of them were maladjusted and delinquent. Yet they had been model pupils for that hour. In the pub at lunchtime, David was quick to point out that he was a mature student with five years experience in a neighbouring school. He also admitted that it was not too difficult to throw a class off balance for a single lesson. Teaching them for a term would require a different approach. Yet he was firmly convinced that a pedagogy which emphasised the mechanics of discipline or which located all the problems of teaching in difficult children was simplistic.

A few of our P.G.C.E. lecturers seemed to know what teaching in Inner-City Schools was like and could be relied on to discuss the difficulties of teaching openly and non-judgementally. We learned almost as much from our discussions with one another. What was seen as maladjusted behaviour in one school, was something teachers in another school had to live with. A disciplinary technique that worked for one teacher did not for another. Classes that had proved difficult for experienced staff were not too bad for us and children who were fine for the regular teachers were a problem in our lessons. It gradually became clear that one child's disruptive behaviour had to be seen within the context of the whole school ethos, the particular classroom relationships and the teachers' behaviour. Bad lessons on teaching practice were not just the fault of the difficult class or the maladjusted individual.

Indeed, the more we thought about concepts like maladjustment, disruptiveness and disaffection, the less meaning they seemed to have. Official definitions seemed contradictory, too. In their Isle of Wight survey, which the Warnock Committee subsequently used for their estimate of Special Needs, Rutter, Tizard and Whitmore (1970) extensively criticised the term "maladjusted":

> most definitions have included the need for treatment... and its chief purpose has been to provide a label under which Special Education has been provided ... the concept of maladjusted has proved to be of regrettably little value in the planning of services.

Many very difficult children seemed to avoid the labelling process and stay in ordinary schools. Furthermore, there was little evidence that those who were sent to special schools fared any better than those who stayed.

One way round these problems of meaning and assessment is provided by Behaviour Modification. It can be used with equal effectiveness in ordinary and special schools and does not require the teacher to make any judgement of how disturbed a child is or why he does what he does. Several P.G.C.E courses now include lectures, videos and practical demonstrations of this approach. Ideally, one would prefer teachers who use Behaviour Modification to carry out these demonstrations and answer questions about them, as the initial response of many people starting to teach is highly suspicious. They may feel that the authority of the teacher ought to be sufficient to make every child behave properly in every situation and that positive reinforcement is no different from bribery. Many behaviourists have followed B. F. Skinner (1953) in talking about their approach as if it were a science, and it is a short step from arguing that operant conditioning can make some human actions predictable, to assuming that we have no free will at all. Skinner's philosophical position is both more complex and more humane than this. He suggests that one of the basic assumptions of psychology is that we have less free will than we suppose. Underpinning his approach is the concept of probability:

> It is a great advantage to suppose that there is a probability that a response will occur... We can then deal with the variables which make the occurence more probable.

Positive attention, praise and material reinforcers can be included amongst these "variables" and he would maintain that they are often more effective than the stock responses of parents and teachers, tellings off and punishments. Furthermore, he would argue that we can know how effective they are by making objective assessments of behaviour before and after the modifiers have been used.

In its pure form, one observes the behaviour of the child over a specific period - say half an hour - and at given intervals - three or four times a week. One notes down all the kinds of behaviour which make teaching or learning difficult. These may range from walking around when the class is meant to be seated, calling out when they are meant to be quiet, and refusing to talk when there is a discussion, to upsetting tables and chairs, hitting other children or banging one's own head on the wall. One notes how often these acts take place and what seems to be setting them off. One child with a history of grand mal epilepsy took to faking these fits at lunchtime in his special school. It seemed apparent that he had his largest audience at these times and that he enjoyed disrupting everyone else's meal. So in this case, his programme of behaviour modification included his having to eat in isolation for a time.

Though it is not strictly necessary to consult the child, many teachers discuss their observations and draw up a "contract". (Krumboltz and Thoresen). A short list of the most disruptive behaviours is compiled and the child promises to reduce them. Then the teacher makes a list of the child's positive behaviours and promises to reward them. The schedule of reinforcements may then be discussed. At first, it is often best to make checks on behaviour frequently and at regular intervals, such as once every two minutes, but the gaps can be extended and then made irregular. The menu of reinforcers can range from regular on the spot praise for work well done, to privileges like being allowed a five minute break at the end of a lesson, to material rewards like sweets or a cup of coffee at the end of a week. One older boy with a history of violent temper tantrums, transferred to an ordinary school from the disruptive unit of a special school, preferred a letter home every week, telling his father how well he had settled in. The contract may have a specific time limit like two to three weeks, at the end of which there will be another behavioural analysis. Generally speaking, some of the deviant behaviours will have been "extinguished", whilst others are lessoned. A new contract may be negotiated, targeting other problems and varying the reinforcers.

It is often argued that with a large class to teach and manage, the teacher cannot afford the time to make detailed and regular checks of one individual. Furthermore, rewarding a child who is normally difficult simply for improving his behaviour may have a destablizing effect on the rest of the class. They may be jealous and may assume that the best way to get extra attention and rewards is by playing up. With large groups, teachers often run what is known as a "token economy" (Ayllon and Azrin). Instead of giving reinforcers there and then, the teacher puts ticks in his register and then a certain number of ticks can be cashed in for the reinforcer at the end of a lesson, or after a private interview at the end of the week. The advantage of this approach is that the difficult child is not singled out for too much individual attention in the classroom itself. With one child, whose disruptive actions included banging his head on the floor and walls, suddenly falling off his chair as if he had fainted, swearing, fighting and calling out when the teacher had the rest of the class listening quietly, we ran a token economy. This also included a child whose behaviour was quiet and conformist but who was terribly inhibited about writing. When members of the class asked what this was about, we told them this was a way of helping anyone who had difficulties settling down in the class. If anyone else wanted to join in they need only ask.

It is argued that by reinforcing desirable behaviour and ignoring the undesirable, one will be more effective than if one assumes that children will behave well and only respond to his behaviour. Some Special Needs Departments and Special Schools set great store by ignoring poor behaviour. Where behaviours are so disruptive, they cannot be ignored in class, spaces are set aside where children can be sent for "time out". Here they receive no attention and no stimulus at all. Where a programme is carefully thought out, it can have dramatic effects on anti-social behaviour and is much more reliable than traditional discipline or counselling. Unless one is asked to use it as part of a team, one needs to be cautious about it at the start of one's career. Kuypers, Becker and O'Leary give an all too plausible account of individual teachers trying to go it alone and having very little effect on their pupils. A child who is in your lesson for two hour-long lessons a week is unlikely to be deeply influenced by a programme designed to lessen calling out in class if, as he feels, "Everybody else does it in all the other subjects I have". Putting a child outside the classroom door as a form of "time out" may infringe school policy, especially where there are groups of children roaming the corridors.

Even when behaviour modification is not employed, there are a number of aspects of it which can be of use to the starting teacher. Firstly behavioural analysis may well be time-consuming and ultimately subjective, but it can give one a clearer idea of what it is that individuals are doing which stops them getting the most out of the lesson or spoils it for others. Discussing these actions calmly and objectively with the child may in itself be of help. Some children who feel that teachers are continually picking on them and that this gives them the right to muck about may be surprised to find out that they have wandered out of their seat three times in half an hour, been involved in a fight, answered back and raised their voice to the teacher. The discussion may then lead to an oral contract. The teacher may say that it is the fighting and raising of his voice that must stop. If he, the teacher, promises not to pick on the child for these things then the child will have to promise not to do them. From now on the teacher will remind the pupil to behave at the beginning of every lesson and then try not to pick on him.

Another aspect of behaviour modification that can be of use is the token economy. One teacher spent "writing lessons", walking round the classroom, putting ticks against the names of all those who were working well. It allowed him the opportunity to spend time looking at the work of every individual, but it also made the class feel that how they behaved was being carefully monitored. At the end of the lesson, the teacher would read out the names of those who got a lot of ticks, providing on the spot praise for good behaviour.

Whilst this kind of unrelenting and methodical checking makes some teachers (and pupils) feel that behaviour modification is close to the custodial, its emphasis on positive reinforcement rather than punishment deserves wider recognition. Making a determined effort to find something one can praise in children who disrupt one's lessons can make a difference not just to their behaviour but to the ethos of the whole class. It is easier said than done, though. It can be salutory to open one's mark book during a lesson and make a note of every child to whom one talks. Those who are just asked statements of fact receive a nought, those we praise get a tick and those we tell off or speak about negatively get a cross. The most striking thing about this kind of check is that we only ever talk to a minority in the class. Negative remarks outnumber positive. And a few children get many more negative remarks than all the rest. Even if one makes a special effort, it is difficult to increase the positive or to talk to more children. It is often said that Secondary School pupils should know how to behave and that the teacher is only responding to the misbehaviour of the few. But it could be argued that if the Warnock Committee's inclusion of "maladjusted" children and those with "social and emotional" difficulties among those with "special educational needs" means anything at all, then it is part of the teacher's responsibility to break into the vicious circle of difficult behaviour and negative reinforcement. Classes where a large number of children feel that they and their efforts are respected by their teacher often seem to be calmer, more buoyant, less bored and less likely to be disrupted than those where it is taken for granted that they should behave properly.

Another kind of approach which is used with troubled and troublesome pupils is Counselling. Many P.G.C.E. courses include options in Guidance and Counselling on the grounds that every teacher needs these skills in order to carry out his duties as a form tutor. There are several problems with this, however. Firstly, there is considerable debate about whether counselling is a skill that can be taught. Success rates vary enormously between counsellors and it is often argued that human warmth, sensitivity and integrity are more important than the length and type of training. Secondly, it seems to be rather more effective when used with pupils who are withdrawn or anxious than acting out and anti-social. And thirdly, there is a feeling that the non-judgemental aspects of counselling undermine the role of teacher. Baroness Warnock herself has drawn attention to the blurring of the differences between social work and teaching and to the way that this has contributed to the loss of status in the profession (Dimbleby Lecture : 1985). Speakers at recent union conferences have emphasised that teachers should confine themselves to imparting knowledge and keeping order and that "those pupils who prevent teachers from teaching should be removed from the classroom" (Peter Matthews : NAS President : reported in T.E.S. 27 : 4 : 84).

There is little doubt, however, that there are children who are in such difficulties that they need extra support, if they are to get the best out of their education. The outside agencies - social workers, home-school liaison workers, psychologists and educational welfare officers - are not always available to help the starting teacher. They tend to work with Pastoral Team Leaders and Special Needs staff in Secondary Schools, rather than at the subject teacher level. It is rare for students on teaching practice or probationers to have an opportunity to discuss their pupils' difficulties with them. Any training on an initial teaching course is of necessity introductory and there are few opportunities to work through the role conflicts of teacher and counsellor. Yet the processes involved in teaching a slow learner to read, write and communicate the basics in arithmetic are so analogous to counselling that the experience of one illuminates the other.

Individual counselling was seen as part of the work of the Special Needs Department on my teaching practice. There was a great deal of support, both through our weekly after school meetings and informal staffroom conversations, and we students were invited to take on one or two pupils. At first the realisation that in the Special Needs class there were pupils who were feeling suicidal, who were victims of child abuse or whose siblings were dying was overwhelming. Even in the ordinary classes, there were large numbers of pupils whose parents were splitting up, or had been faced with long term unemployment and poverty. In an Inner-City area like this, it was estimated that one fifth of the boys had police records. And the first few attempts at counselling made one feel powerless to help. A bright and lively school leaver, who had hardly been to school since he was eight and could barely read, said he had spent his weekend "knocking off" parking meters. He and his friends had been hitting the top of the meter with a hammer until it came off the pole, then emptying the cash box. Knowing that counselling involved confidentiality and that one should be warm and non-judgemental I just listened, but I honestly felt that if what this boy was telling me was true, it was wrong and should be reported. It was only a couple of years later when told of more serious offences involving burglary and firearms that one felt one had to discuss this problem with a psychologist and set limits to confidentiality. One needs to feel sufficiently secure in one's relationship with the pupils to warn them that if they tell one anything illegal or dangerous to themselves or others, one may well have to pass on the information. At the time, however, I felt confused and ambivalent, and sensing this the boy did not return for further sessions.

The atmosphere of the teaching practice school's Special Needs Department was such that one felt one could discuss every aspect of teaching with them, including the failures. Through our seminars and informal chats one gradually learned more about the pupils, about oneself and about the listening process - essential in both reading and counselling. One of the most satisfying things that happened on that term was being given a poem by one of our lowest attainers about what it felt like to learn to read. The pupil concerned was a recent emigrant from Guyana. In the previous lesson we had stopped our reading and he told me about the grandparents and brothers he had left behind, about the school he had hardly attended and the sense of cold he had felt since arriving in England. His eyes watered and he kept blowing his nose. One felt one was listening to the very language of exile. There was a pause and he fell silent. Just as in the reading lesson, when a child is stuck, the teacher goes back over the last few words, recapitulating them so that the child is reminded of the meaning of the passage; so in the counselling situation, one used the silence to reflect back to the client the meaning of what he had just been saying. In a sense this was easy, for my own experience in that school was still raw.

The simple clarification of a problem by a sympathetic adult allows the child to come to terms with it. The reformulation appears to lessen the sense of distress. In the case of this child, he then said that the one bright spot in coming to England was learning to read. It was this opportunity to explain the events of the past few months to himself and an adult who wanted to listen that led to this poem, his first piece of free writing.

There are many competing schools and perspectives in Counselling, Rogerian, Transactional Analysis and others, which can be explored in greater depth through one's career. Some Colleges and Universities have in-service courses and many teachers also train for the Samaritans and Marriage Guidance Council. Again and again one meets failure. Equally there are pupils across the whole ability range for whom a few counselling sessions can make a significant difference, educationally and in their wider social and emotional development. In the same fourth year class, there were two girls with apparently similar childhood experiences and present behavioural problems. Tracy was a child from a single parent family. Her mother was alcoholic and she had spent several periods in a mental hospital. Tracy had endured several separations in early childhood and then been fostered. The fostering itself broke down several times in early adolescence and each time this happened Tracy had also had to change schools. She was of average ability and yet her attainments were at the Special Needs level. At about the time of her previous fostering she had been close to expulsion from school. She was also in trouble with the police. Just before the last foster placement broke down, and she left our school, she seemed on the verge of coming to terms with her lack of trust in adults, but could not take the final step. She said, "I like you but I'm not on your side. I don't care."

In the same class as Tracy, there was another girl called Pamela. She had also had many changes of school and her parents had separated. She also found it very hard to trust adults and she had been suspended from a previous school for theft, bullying and gross defiance. She had a hard, aggressive exterior and was surprised to find herself in tears in one counselling session as she looked back over her childhood. Her father had walked out when she was eight. Shortly afterwards she had had to spend a long time in hospital and she had thought her mother had deserted her too. Her mother had been briefly married to a man who had knocked both Pamela and her mother about. Since then there had been a long history of battles and rejections at home and at school. A few weeks after these conversations, Pamela reported that she had begun to enjoy her lessons for the first time in her life. She even liked three or four of her teachers. She came top in several of her end of year exams and got a special commendation from the Headmaster.

Even from teaching practice, it was made quite clear that while a successful counselling relationship helps one to win the affection of an individual child, it does not necessarily make for an easier life as a classroom teacher. Pupils are not just difficult with teachers they dislike. Unresolved conflicts between one's desire to be available to children in distress and one's need to keep control will be exploited. Both the girls described above were difficult to manage and as transference developed in the counselling situation, the more they expected the teacher to keep them in line in the classroom. Learning to maintain high standards of behaviour from troublesome children, even though one understands and sympathises with their problems, is not easy.

Issues like the sense of failure one feels when a relationship breaks down or the risks one runs in trying to be both firm and sympathetic can only be discussed in an atmosphere of trust. In my teaching practice school, the Special Needs Department provided this. While it would be grossly unfair to suggest that all the children with behavioural problems are taught by Special Needs staff or that all those with Special Needs are difficult, the fact that Special Needs Departments often work with small groups and are used to giving lots of individual attention may make them a place to which students or probationary teachers can turn to for help and support.

In my own probationary school, Heads of Department encouraged young teachers to observe each others' classes and meet after school to discuss curricular and disciplinary issues. Quite a few schools have induction programmes which go beyond explaining how to take a register and where to apply for extra books. They provide an opportunity for this sort of mutual support. More and more now, when falling rolls mean that each school only has a new teacher every two or three years. Advisers bring probationary teachers from groups of schools together with experienced pastoral staff, lecturers in counselling and psychologists so that that they can discuss common problems. For many staff, dealing with difficult children brings out feelings which one would rather not have to admit. Anger and fear can in themselves induce anxiety and guilt. The bluster and shouting at the front of a class may not be real anger, but the teacher feels that this is uncomfortably near the surface. Sensing this, difficult pupils play him up to see how much he will take before he "goes mad". Open discusion of emotional experiences of teaching makes one realize how common they are. Clarification by a group leader can then lead to a greater sense of self acceptance.

One of the ideas that emerged in these discussions in my own probationary year was that we should aim for the least disruptive forms of teacher intervention. We were all aware of how punishing a child, a sudden shout or an outburst of temper from the teacher created a ripple effect. The class as a whole would go quiet and for a short period it would seem as if the air had been cleared. Too many sudden interruptions, however, seemed to make the pupils restless. The children themselves complained that we were shouting so much that they could not get on with their work. Some of us observed that teachers who appeared to have the least trouble from disruptive pupils rarely seemed to shout or punish, and that when they did so, it was only after the class had been clearly warned in advance. There may be times when we had to be angry with a pupil, but we decided we should try to keep these to a minimum. What we decided was this. We would not shout when a telling off would suffice. We would not tell a child off when we could simply explain what he was doing wrong. We would not give a long explanation, when walking determinedly towards his desk would do. We would attempt to manage the class so far as possible with quick visual checks, by waiting for a class to be silent and by using our sense of humour. Some advisers have videos of teachers using just these techniques, showing that if a teacher can keep a class "steady" by merely looking, waiting for silence and "having a laugh", the class as a whole works more evenly and the supposedly difficult children are less apparent.

In a questionnaire one probationer worked out

about how his Social Studies classes perceived good discipline, we found that it was not the teachers who shouted most often or most loudly whom the children most respected, it was those who gave them good warning that they were getting angry. Mr Grey had excellent control. Most of the time he had a good laugh with you. He explained what you had to do very clearly and his lab. was always well organized. If the class went "too far", he went red in the face. Everybody knew they had to behave then, because if they put a foot out of line the teacher was sure to lose his temper.

Tips for teachers, like the minimalization of negative interventions, the use of praise and so on do not work for everyone. Where one may want to relax and learn to enjoy his classes more, another may need to be more assertive. Children's perceptions of what makes a good teacher are often paradoxical. The two quoted below were discussing Miss Black. They thought she was excellent at managing difficult pupils. One of the most notorious girls in the school said she had been a "right terror" until she had had Miss Black in the Third Year as a form tutor. She had a knack of making everyone feel O.K., even first thing in the morning, but that did not mean she was "soft":

Rory : She can be all right. You can have a laugh with her, like ... Well she's not like everybody else. It's not like you're all tensed up. You can talk a bit but if it's too noisy, she'll give you lines or detention or something.

Jenny: She says she'll give you lines but she doesn't always. They don't know if they're going to be let off, not until the end. She shouts at you sometimes and keeps you in suspense.

The experienced teachers to whom this tape has been played doubted whether they could get away with letting pupils off punishments, but Miss Black apparently does so, while maintaining the image of a teacher who can be strict if she wants to be. In my own probationary year, the children in one class told me that I was not strict enough, but that I shouted too much. I explained that it was their misbehaviour that made me shout, and that anyway it made no sense that I should be tougher on them and yet tell them off less. Their advice was sound, however paradoxical it sounded and over the next few weeks I made a determined effort to follow it. One of them was appointed "shouting monitor", so that we had an independent observer. At first it was difficult not to give way to frustration and at the same time to devise alternative ways of keeping control. Though behaviour patterns in the most difficult children had already been established, it did seem as if the quieter atmostphere was making them marginally less disturbed.

The gradual deterioration in relations between the Government, L.E.A.'s and classroom teachers has contributed quite considerably to an increase in behavioural problems. Pupils banned from schools during the lunchbreak came back over-excited, strikes have encouraged truancy and there is a pervasive feeling that no-one cares what happens to young people. Teachers who for years have run football teams, school orchestras or canoeing trips for disadvantaged children have dropped their out-of-school activities., They are more overtly cynical towards their pupils and are offering much less support to starting teachers. Lecturers without regular school teaching commitments appear unaware of the depth of demoralisation and those on teaching practice or a probationary year may not know if there is anyone to whom they can turn for help and support.

Nevertheless there are techniques one can learn and people who can show one how to be a more effective teacher of difficult children. Despite the unfashionability of going beyond the imparting of knowledge and discipline, there is still something implicit in our notions of a "good teacher" which includes the ability to manage troubled and troublesome children warmly, caringly and unflappably. Beginning teachers who start out by aiming to get the best out of difficult children bring something richer to their teaching of less demanding children. Learning to deal with extremes, both in terms of learning abilities and behaviour gives one a greater degree of flexibility and humanity with the broad mass of pupils. The view that difficult children should simply be removed from our classrooms is both shallow and unrealistic.

REFERENCES

Ayllon, T. and Azrin, N. (1968) The Token Economy : A Motivational System for Therapy and Rehabilitation : Appleton Century Crofts
Krumboltz, J.D. and Thoresen, C.E. (1969) Behavioural Counselling : Holt Rinehart and Winston
Kuypers, D.S., Becker, W.C. and O'Leary, K.D. (1968) How to Make a Token System Fail : in Exceptional Children : v 35 : 101-9
Rutter, M., Tizard, J. and Whitmore, K. (1970) Education, Health and Behaviour : Longman
Skinner, B.F. (1953) Science and Human Behaviour : MacMillan
Warnock, H.M. (1985) Dimbleby Lecture

FURTHER READING

Berne, E. (1978) Games People Play : Ballantine
Carkhuff, R.R. and Berenson, B.G. (1977) Beyond Counselling and Therapy : Holt Rinehart and Winston
Corrigan, P. (1979) Schooling the Smash Street-Kids: MacMillan
Eysenck, H.J. (1952) The effects of Psycholotherapy An Evaluation : Journal of Consulting Psychology : 16 : 4 : 319-327
Fischer, J. et al (1975) Relationship between Theoretical Orientation and Therapist's Empathy, Warmth and Genuineness : Journal of Consulting Psychology : 22 : 394-403
Gillham, W.E.C. (1978) Reconstructing Educational Psychology : Croom Helm
Galloway, D. et al (1982) Schools and Disruptive Pupils : Longman
Hargreaves, D.H. et al (1975) Deviance in Classrooms : Routledge
Laslett, R. and Smith, C. (1984) Effective Classroom Management: Croom Helm
Morrison, A. and McIntyre, D. (1972) The Social Psychology of Teaching : Penguin
Kounin, J.S. (1970) Discipline and Group Management in Classrooms : Holt Rinehart and Winston
Power, M.J. et al (1967) Delinquent Schools? New Society : 19 : 10 : 67
Rogers, C.R. : Client Centred Therapy : Houghton Miffin
Salzberger-Wittenburg, I. et al (1983) The Emotional Experience of Learning and Teaching: Routledge and Kegan Paul

Chapter Eight

PARENTS AND THE COMMUNITY

In a discussion about home-school links, one student said that during her teaching practice, the teachers in her Primary School used to gather at the staffroom window every morning, watching parents bring their children to school. They would make cutting remarks about how parents treated their children or how they were dressed. They were particularly scathing about the parents of those who gave them the most trouble, those with learning or behavioural difficulties. The teacher whose class this student had taken over did not want her to invite parents into the school, and there was no school policy about helping parents to assist their children's education.

Christine, the student, contrasted this with the policy of the special school where her mother worked. Not only were there regular meetings for all parents, individual parents were encouraged to drop in and see staff informally. A few worked alongside the professionals, hearing children read or assisting with cookery, needlework and craft. Christine and another student friend had also been allowed to take groups of children during College vacations and she had found this practice in teaching more interesting than some that the College had organized.

There is tremendous diversity in relationships between schools and the parents of children with Special Needs. Occasionally one comes across children with quite marked disabilities who are attaining at exceptionally high levels. These cases often reveal long-term involvement by parents who have read widely about their children's problems and even attended courses on Special Needs. These parents may well take the lead in developing a partnership between themselves and schools,inviting homework and holiday projects, welcoming hints about their involvement in decision making and joining Case Conferences as equals.

Some schools have themselves initiated this shared approach. There have been reading drives in which parents are invited to Special Consultation evenings to show them how they can be of help and which the teachers then follow up with home visits. It is astonishing how much difference these can make. After one such programme where the parents of First Year Secondary School children had been shown how to help them practice, we found that they made 50% more progress than we would have expected. Motivation improved and the pupils appeared to settle into their new school more quickly, too. Parents can even assist when children have quite marked problems. Children following the rigorously programmed DISTAR approach (Engelmann et al) are given "Take Homes". And those using language experience can be helped with "paired reading." In this, parent and child sit together with a single book and the child points to each word as he is ready to read it. At first parents read every word with the child, so there is no pressure on children about having to get everything correct. Reading alongside someone else helps them comprehend and use the meaning as an additional one. Gradually the parent reads less and less. The child has to tap on a word for the parent to help. If the child makes lots of mistakes and is in a muddle, the parent simply reads the passage back to him. Small scale research on paired reading has shown very encouraging results and we found that one boy, who had been stuck at a reading age of six despite five years of individual help by professional Special Needs staff, suddenly made two years progress after his parents had been shown the technique. This boy, Colin, had been brought up in considerable poverty and it had simply been assumed that the parents were unable to help. But the motivation to read now that his father was helping him made a huge difference. Even in other areas of the curriculum like Maths and History, we saw a new interest and a determination to catch up.

All too often, however, particularly in ordinary schools where children with Special Needs are in a minority and not subject to regular formal review, contacts are more patchy. Parents of children with Special Needs come only rarely to formal parents evenings, and school policy may not encourage home visiting. The parents will say that they are often made to feel failures themselves because of their children's difficulties. And they feel embarrassed talking about them in a large classroom or school hall, with other parents listening.

For their part, there are a few teachers who are openly intolerant of such children and their parents. Unhappily, the present problems between teachers and the government have made more and more say that their professional contract only concerns what happens inside school and during school hours. If parents will not come into school, that is their affair. The Warnock Report on Special Educational Needs saw this quite differently. They suggested that the integration of handicapped children and the more effective teaching of children with Special Needs depended on much closer cooperation between home and school:

> We have insisted throughout this report that the successful education of children with special educational needs is dependent upon the full involvement of their parents : indeed, unless the parents are seen as equal partners in the educational process the purpose of our report will be frustrated.

Learning how much parents can help the teacher is something which can start during the P.G.C.E. and probationary year. My own probationary school encouraged all staff to ensure that parents in their tutor groups came to consultation evenings and to visit parents in their own homes. Many parents in that Inner-City area worked late afternoon or evening shifts. The father of one boy did not finish until after nine o'clock. He was desperately concerned about his son's behaviour in school and would have liked to have talked it over with all his teachers, but he could not afford to miss the whole shift. For a beginning teacher, with an upbringing as sheltered as mine, such visits could be extremely illuminating. Just to hear this father talk about the fairly minor infringement of the rules at home and see the belt he used to punish his son with made one realize why he should be having problems with my own more liberal classroom regime.

Occasionally, meetings with parents had a way of making one question the theories one had picked up on College courses about the causes of learning difficulties. Simon was one of the most difficult pupils in my tutor group. He threw temper tantrums very easily and if one attempted to restrain him physically he fought back. He was capable of throwing over all the desks in a classroom and once when he was put out of a lesson into the corridor, he loosened the polystyrene tiles in the false ceiling and smashed them into pieces. If you spoke to him while he was still very upset, he would talk about himself in the third person "Simon is very sorry for what he done". Despite all this, a lot of teachers wanted to help him and when, at the end of a day, he had been excluded from lessons and was waiting to be taken home by his year tutor yet again, I asked if I could go with him.

The family lived in two rooms and Simon was the middle of three children. When he was about six, his mother had taken his elder brother from Jamaica to England, leaving him with a rather elderly grandmother. He had always been a difficult baby, but now the tantrums he threw were too much for grandmother or school to cope with. At her wits' ends, she persuaded Simon's mother to take him. There was now a younger brother, too and Simon was bitterly jealous. He had spent less than a year at Primary School and having barely settled there, he transferred to Secondary.

Not only did this visit help me to understand why Simon acted the way he did, it also made one question a concept which is frequently used to explain the poor attainments of working class and ethnic minority children - linguistic deprivation. Simon's mother had a gift for words and she brought vividly to life what Simon had undergone. She made one realize that Simon too used Jamaican patois with a vitality which made other children's standard English seem poor and dull. Yet pupils were hardly allowed to use it at school. As a result of these visits and conversations with other staff, it became clear that much of the literature and Special Needs reading material in the school was inadequate. Not only did we have few stories from the Third World, those we used often treated blacks as outsiders and made their language seem strange and ungrammatical. Some of us started to encourage pupils to write long autobiographies in a range of different styles and produced our own material. To have transliterated Jamaican speech sounds would have underlined their foreignness, so we wrote in dialect and transliterated the English of the whites who appeared in the stories.

One was typed and sent to publishers, it

circulated in the class and a professional photographer came to the school to put some of the scenes on film. The effect of reflecting the pupil's own language back to them and trying to crystalize some of their experiences was tremendous. It gave them a huge amount of confidence. The willingness of the class to write and express their own ideas and feelings redoubled. Simon and his mother were not helped however and, after drifting from one special school to another, he ended up in a residential placement.

The parents of handicapped children often have a wealth of knowledge and experience to share with their teachers, if we will only listen. A home visit to the parents of a partially sighted child appeared to get off to a bad start when she told me how often she had complained to the school and how little had been done. On the first day at the Comprehensive, there had been a Maths test. Unfortunately it was duplicated in blue ink and some of the final copies had been faded. Chris, her son, could not read his and despite a letter, she had found that he had been given similar worksheets time and time again. One teacher even used blue duplicating masters and light blue paper. She wanted her son treated the same as everyone else, but though the school said they understood his problems, most of Chris' teachers were reluctant to punish him. She thought that the idea of shouting at a blind boy upset them. While they would do it to the others in Chris' class, they seemed unwilling to do it to him. Despite her own visual difficulties, she was studying for an Open University degree and she knew that Chris could have done a lot better than he was doing.

Another mother, whose child's spelling and word attack skills were a long way behind her comprehension and general intelligence said that she was sure Michelle's hearing was poor. She herself had noticed that Michelle missed what people said before she started school. The school doctor had noticed nothing and none of her teachers had asked for a subsequent test or done anything to place her at the front of the class. She did not know whom to turn to. When we contacted the peripatetic service for the hearing impaired, we found that she had a hearing loss of 45 db. Though this would have been seen as a mild handicap, it would have meant that she would have had frequent difficulty with speech at normal loudness. In early childhood Michelle had had lots of ear infections and catarrh and these would have exacerbated the problems from time to time. No special strategies had been devised for helping her reading or wider language development, and yet her mother had known "something was wrong" all the time.

It is not only the parents of children with physical or sensory disabilities who can help the teacher. The mother of one of lowest attaining school leavers said that Robin's work had been getting worse since he was eleven. According to our records, Robin's father was an agricultural labourer, all the other children had left school illiterate and Robin had been stuck at a reading age of seven. Mother was extremely nervous and defensive at the start of the visit, assuming that it concerned Robin's truancy. She needed considerable reassurance before she could be told that Robin was receiving extra individual assistance and that we would appreciate her help. Eventually she was mollified and then she said that Robin had been able to read a newspaper when he left Junior School. He had made mistakes, especially with names of people he did not know, but he always got the gist of what he was reading.

This tallied with our experience exactly. Robin often managed to grasp the underlying meaning of a passage even when it was supposedly beyond his reading ability. He could guess words in context but his nervousness often created problems for him at the surface level. He reversed letters, omitted words, jumped from line to line and jumbled words that had more than two syllables. We had been getting progress by refusing to correct or criticise and merely praising him for every line he read perfectly. If we were remotely critical of his reading, he either became belligerent or grew very nervous and made more mistakes. After his mother told us that Robin had been able to read better previously, we agreed that this knowledge would enable her to give Robin a lot more confidence. If she pulled him up on his errors, he might take it more easily than he would from us. She saw what we were driving at and agreed to help.

For a few weeks after that, she made Robin sit down with her for a reading lesson every night before the older children and her husband got home from work. Using books and reading teaching techniques which we suggested, she helped him to make rapid progress. There was another short visit a little later and she said how his improvement in reading had helped Robin in a range of other unforeseen ways. He was a C.B. fan and having contacted another fan two or three hundred miles away, he had arranged a holiday there for himself, something for which he would never have had the confidence previously.

Not all parents are as good at helping their children as that, and there is an ethical problem involved with older pupils. Many would prefer to keep home and school separate and feel that if their parents ever found out how weak their school work was, they would be ashamed of them. Some parents would like to help, but when it comes to it, they do not have the patience. One thirteen year old called Minette was desperate to read and we talked over the possibility of asking her step mother to help. Minette knew she would like to, but somehow thought she might "get in a state". This in fact happened, and in a follow up home visit, Minette's step mother admitted that after a good start, they had both ended in tears every night. They had been told that if this happened they should give up at once, but they had both felt driven to carry on.

Even where this does happen, there is a great deal that successful home-school relations can do to help. Maria was an intelligent, attractive and sophisticated fourteen year old with specific learning difficulties. That is to say, there was a marked difference between her IQ and her attainments. She had an IQ of 120 and a reading age of eight. Her spelling was indecipherable and she often has difficulty reading back what she herself has written. Maria's parents were very concerned. They realized that if only she could read she would be clever enough to take 'O' levels. As things stood, however, she was in bottom sets for every subject, unable even to shine at Maths because she could not read the textbook. They would have liked to help with homeworks. Not only did this make Maria's mother very upset, Maria herself could not always read back her homework assignments.

Maria's parents came to the school to see what they could do. We had been able to talk over their sense of frustration, the fear of being thought a pushy or hysterical parent, the very real anger they felt when a teacher who has been told that their child has specific learning difficulties shouts at her in class. "Can't you read <u>that</u>! You must be blind or something'" One could not discuss these kinds of problems in an open school hall at a parents' evening, so one of the staff with a nearby office was asked beforehand if it could be used for private discussions. Progress in Maria's case was slow, but she eventually left school with a range of C.S.E.'s.

There are others from the school and wider community who can also be of help. Many Comprehensives ask their Sixth Formers to help out during registration or private study periods, and it may be that teaching backward readers is what leads some of them into the profession. Sixth Formers not only hear children read, they can help out in a hands-on computer lessons and in Maths. A few Sixth Forms also set up links with special schools or Ph AB clubs, encouraging closer ties between ordinary schools and handicapped children, even where the education system as a whole seems to be drifting further and further away from integration.

It is also quite common for teachers of older "non-exam" groups to send their pupils to help out with children who have Special Needs in Primary Schools. This needs to be carefully arranged, as some Primary teachers are unused to working with adolescents and have little idea how poor their attainments can be. There are pupils in Top Infants whose reading, writing and Maths are more competent than some school leavers. Many non-exam child care and communication skills courses include elements on language development. Successful practical work like hearing children read and writing books for the very young can help the leavers' self-confidence and social skills.

Many countries do far more than us to involve the community. In Denmark the degree of integration among children and adolescents means that the handicapped are much more accepted as adults. Their unemployment rates are no higher than the general populations, despite the lack of legally enforced employment quotas. In the Soviet Union, where most classes are taught on a mixed ability basis through to 16, classmates are expected to help those who fall behind. Teachers provide extra lessons as a matter of course, and schools are in regular contact with parents to ensure that those with problems keep up. Although it is difficult to be sure about this, informal evidence indicates that attainments among the less able are considerably higher than we achieve (Grant : Segal). In the United States, there are summer camps for disabled and low attaining pupils, where students are paid to act as the equivalent of youth workers. Teachers are paid to undertake Vacation courses on "exceptional children". Many of the initiatives which led to the placing of Federal obligations to set up programmes and reviews for these children came about after parents brought boards of education to court in pursuit of their children's constitutional rights. (Dunn)

There are those who believe that the 1981 Education Act has made it possible for parents to put more pressure on L.E.A.'s about adequate special provision in ordinary schools and segregation. If we are to see marked changes of attitude towards the underachievement of those with learning difficulties and the wider acceptance of the handicapped, it may well come about through the partnership of parents and teachers. For staff who are concerned, parents are natural allies. Not only do they shed light on individuals' needs and correct our prejudices, they remind us of the intolerance still to be overcome.

REFERENCES

Dunn, L.M. (1973) Exceptional Children in the Schools : Holt, Rinehart and Winston
Engelmann, Carnine and Johnson (1978) DISTAR
Grant, N. (1979) Soviet Education : Penguin
Segal, S.S. (1966) Backward Children in the USSR : Arnold

FURTHER READING

Anderson, E.M. et al (1982) Disability in Adolescence : Methuen
Bagley and Verma (1983) Multicultural Childhood: Gower
Barton, L. and Tomlinson, S. (1982) Special Education : Policy, Practices and Social Issues : Harper and Row
Boswell, D.M. and Wingrove, J.M. (1974) The Handicapped Person in the Community : O.U
Chapman, E.K. (1978) Visually Handicapped Children and Young People : Routledge and Kegan Paul
Conrad, R. (1979) The Deaf School Child : Harper and Row
Craft, M. et al (1980) Linking Home and School : Harper
Goffman, E. (1963) Stigma : Penguin
Halliwell, M. and Spain, B. (1977) Spina Bifida Children in Ordinary Schools
Hewison, J. and Tizard, J. (1980) Parental Involvement and Reading Attainment : Brit, J. Educ. Psychol : 50 : 209-215
Tansley, P. and Panckhurst, J. 1981 : Children with Specific Learning Difficulties : NFER : Nelson

Chapter Nine

COMPREHENSIVE COMMITMENT

There are times when all teachers complain that there is no point trying to teach certain pupils. One knows one is making little progress and it seems impossible to get through to some of the class. For many teachers this is particularly true of children with Special Needs. Only recently one of the most competent and hard working of colleagues described how absence rates, deteriorating behaviour and lethargy amongst her low ability Fourth Years made her feel it was hardly worthwhile trying to get any work out of them in the last fortnight of term. Even at times when teachers have felt they have had more support from the government and the community, one found that a few of the children in Special Needs classes actually regressed over the years. On my own teaching practice, there were moments when one thought that the only reason why such classes had been created was that their small size and practical curricula provided the easiest way of keeping control over children who had no hopes of educational qualification, jobs or a stake in society.

Some of the critics of the Warnock Report and the legislation that followed it have argued that these ignored crucial issues of labelling and social control. (Lewis and Vulliamy : Tomlinson) There are deep rooted structural problems in the way our society distributes and transmits its cultural and educational opportunities. Some children's language is closer to that of their teachers and textbooks and they also tend to be the one who find the first steps in reading and number easiest. Even from an early age, children seem to know who is doing well and who is not. (Nash) Those who fail to read develop a negative self concept which in turn affects concentration, memory and motivation. In order to qualify for special provision, these children have first to be labelled as having Special Needs. These informal and formal labelling processes deepen their sense of abnormality. These critics would argue that once perceived as having Special Needs, these children often progress to classes where no-one is thought capable of any worthwhile intellectual activity, let alone a job.

The expansion of official definitions of special provision from the 2% of children in special schools to the 20% who are thought to have learning difficulties at some time in their school careers, coincided with a massive increase in youth unemployment. If there is to be a large minority of pupils who can expect short-term unpleasant jobs or no work at all, then special provision and the labelling that accompanies it could provide a social function that goes beyond its overt educational objectives. Special provision could be a way of socialising some of our children into accepting their place in the pool of unemployment and its alternative, doing our society's dirty work.

Sometimes one even meets well intentioned and thoughtful teachers who revel in this role. One described how she had met an ex-pupil recently. Gary had had great difficulties with school work and she had never expected him to have a job. He was covered from head to foot in manure and he told her he had got a job in a Garden Centre. Gary's teacher said that even in the open street, he smelt so foul that she gagged. He was doing a job no one else wanted and being paid a pittance for his pains, but she was proud of him. He might well be ridiculed by friends and family, but she told him she was happy he had found his niche in life.

If the Warnock Report has had little positive effect on employment prospects of pupils with Special Needs, this is scarcely surprising. Educational integration has actually lessened since it was published. Government cut backs have made L.E.A's reluctant to close their special schools. There can be an outcry about the closure of a unit for partially hearing children, but if the same children are scattered in ordinary schools and receiving extra individual attention on site, no-one will make a fuss about the loss of a few hours' teacher time. Special schools have quietly become counters in a political game. Hence, though the numbers of children with special educational needs has fallen as fast as the general population, the proportion of children in special schools actually rose by 4.8% in the 5 years following Warnock. (Swann : 1984)

The government have made commitments and Sir Keith Joseph announced that an expansion in In-Service for Computer Education and Special Needs was a priority on entering office. Short courses have increased notably through the 4/84 scheme, but recruitment in the Secondary Sector has often been limited to experienced teachers already specialising in this work. Progress in initial training has been extremely slow, as we saw in the first chapter, and we are nowhere close even to the very limited training recommendations which Warnock made as its first priority:

i The inclusion of a special education element in all courses of initial training.

ii Short courses on special educational needs of about one week's full-time study or its part-time equivalent to be taken by the great majority of serving teachers.

One has to ask oneself how it is that despite the undoubted difficulties of the work and the dilatory actions of the authorities, teachers still want to learn more about the education of children with Special Needs. A recent survey of in-service training showed that the three areas most likely to attract support were the introduction of new curricula, teaching the less able and behavioural difficulties. (Lynch: 1984).

Working with Special Needs groups can be more satisfying than with able-bodied, average and amenable children. A colleague working with a small group of Third Year pupils, including Maria, the child with specific learning difficulties mentioned in the chapter on Parents, remarked how pleasant it was to be with such adult and perceptive pupils. A writing lesson which had begun with a discussion, which the teacher found refreshingly imaginative and easy, generated essays which were the longest and most ambitious this group had ever done. Problems about spelling and punctuation were raised openly and discussed in the group without sarcasm.

Speaking to a group of students, who had just returned from a long teaching practice, quite a few said that they had got more out of their work in Remedial Departments than they had with their 'O' level groups. It had placed greater demands on their creativity, imagination and personalities. No doubt, further experience with top stream classes would help them to make them as lively as their "slow learners" had been. But the able pupils had had such an instrumental view of education and all many of them wanted was for the teacher to provide them with a good set of notes for the exam. These students also felt that labels like "learning difficulties" and "maladjusted" often turned out to be illusory, once one got to know the children. One did not know how well certain children could do if only they were taught more competently. Children and teachers were caught in a self-fulfilling prophecy, a web of lowered expectations, through which there must be a way of breaking. These students had been astonished again and again by how much the special class had understood and learned. For them, teaching these groups well was a better test of one's educational abilities than steering their 'O' level classes through their exam.

Teaching special groups also allowed one more autonomy. Many of their high and middle sets had clearly laid out syllabi which reached down from 'O' level and C.S.E. to the younger classes. These had to be worked through, however irrelevant they appeared to the children. Younger classes of less able children either had no set syllabus, or the Head of Department was prepared to let a student adapt the existing one. As one said,why work through the school textbook's chapters on Charles I's constitutional crises when a look at ordinary people's lives in this period and a project on the Civil War were more likely to catch the imagination. At the same time as enjoying this freedom, the students thought they would have gained more if there had been greater opportunities to discuss their ideas with lecturers, teachers or peers similarly engaged.

Quite a few of these particular students had asked if they could teach reading on a regular basis during teaching practice. Most of them enjoyed it and thought it shed light on their work with less able pupils in their subject area. They felt that the atmosphere of these smaller reading groups made it possible to get closer to the children and abandon so many of the formal ploys and techniques of the teacher role. They could be less defensive and enjoy the pupils more. This was also true of students who had done some cooperative teaching in their own subjects. The presence of a Special Needs teacher allowed them to spend less time on the custodial aspects of teaching, more time getting to know the children and look at their books as they worked. Small groups and team teaching not only allow one to assess the children in greater depth, they provide beginning teachers with a naturalistic but secure place to experiment with more open relationships.

Learning about Special Needs through college based Warnock "Elements" represents a kind of progress, but it has the danger of generating stereotypes and lowering teacher expectations. If lecturers are teaching in neighbouring comprehensives and can bring in examples of children's work and tapes of their lessons, this would be of help. Even more fruitful is practical experience with small or shared groups. Where the experience of students becomes the starting point for seminar work, it may be possible to overcome the problems of labelling and underachievement.

There is a clear need for an increase in the scope of teacher training in this area. There are doubtless staff in many schools who teach their subjects well to children with learning and behavioural difficulties. But all too often their work is isolated and uncoordinated. Unless we can increase their numbers, and get them to work more closely together, we can have little effect on these pupils' attainments. As long ago as 1948, researchers like Collins were aware that remedial education produced rapid improvements in basic skills, but that when children were put back into their ordinary classrooms, progress slowed. He compared two remedial groups with children who had had similar problems, but no extra help and found two years later that there was no difference between them. Without effective follow up by teachers who understand their children's need and have high expectations of them, remedial education is a "hoax" (Collins : 1971)

More recent research has shown that where a significantly large number of Secondary School staff have had guided practical experience of small group, Special Needs work, there is no such long term fall off. (Sewell : 1982) We recruited subject specialists from across the curriculum, some of whom were probationary teachers, to spend a couple of periods a week in the Special Needs Department. We trained them on site and just gave them a few children to work with. We found that by and large the short term gains these teachers achieved were comparable to those of experienced Special Needs staff. But we also found that simply working with these pupils at close quarters had taught them what children with Special Needs were capable of. They went back into their own areas of the curriculum and generated more appropriate schemes of work, chose textbooks and teaching methods that were more effective. As a result, though progress in the basic skills slowed when remedial provision stopped, it was still sufficient to keep them well ahead of borderline children who had never been included in these groups. We found that where there is a significantly large minority of staff with this experience, and where such teachers work through the age range and across the curriculum, improvements in the children's attainments can be permanent.

Subsequent work has shown that where there is a group of trained and committed staff, children who arrive in a Comprehensive School with Special Needs may leave with qualifications and job prospects that are not significantly different from the rest of the less able 40% of the population. Pupils who previously would not have been thought capable of taking exams may take a range of C.S.E.'s. We found that after three years of the kinds of approaches outlined above, the Grade point average for children who joined the school in Special Needs classes was no worse than many who started in higher streams. Three of our original backward readers even passed C.S.E. English at Grade 4 and all the rest did at Grade 5. Children who said in their second year that they were "too thick to get a job" found work more quickly than some of their supposedly more able peers. While there is little the teacher can do to stop the rising tide of youth unemployment or to counter its effects on pupil morale, one can ensure that disabled children or those with learning or behavioural difficulties, are not socialised into accepting a place in the pool of unemployment or into doing society's dirty work.

One girl, who had constantly been in trouble for fighting lower down the school, wrote in her final report:

> I don't like school. Teachers say school is there to learn but we only come because we have to. School is boring if you are in the

> low sets and that is why you mess around in lessons. I have been in trouble mainly in the fourth year.

She thought that her teachers were always "picking on me, so I shouted back". When she looked at her subjects more closely, though, she began to realize how well she had got on:

> I don't mind Maths. The teacher is nice and the subject is okay as well. I like P.E. especially at the moment. I am playing tennis for my house colour. In the first and second year I didn't like doing games because I was fat. English is the best. There is lots to do and there is a variety of things to do.

Janet concluded that school had prepared her well for leaving school and that some of her most useful lessons had been in Personal Care and Careers:

> I liked the teacher because he taught me to think positive.

One can see quite clearly in Janet's case that the use of praise, more appropriate curricula and a relaxed attitude among a group of her teachers had helped her overcome the feeling that she was incapable of worthwhile educational achievement or employment. Given satisfactory practical experience and the opportunity to discuss it, a larger proportion of teachers could be encouraged to learn how to be more effective with slow learners, the difficult and the handicapped from the start of their careers. The problem about whether young teachers should confine themselves to "normal" pupils and later, when they had experience and expertise, move onto those with Special Needs, has been overtaken by the increased use of mixed ability groups and the increasing demand that all children should follow the same curriculum. We still have a great deal to learn about what constitutes an appropriate curriculum, but these issues are common to all teachers. There is no doubt that all who work in Comprehensive Schools can expect to teach children with Special Needs, so as Gerry, the student quoted in the first chapter, suggested, there is much to be gained by making the P.G.C.E. year an opportunity for the shared: "exploration of our experiences."

REFERENCES

Collins, J.E. (1961) The Effects of Remedial Education : Oliver and Boyd

Collins, J.E. (1971) The Remedial Reading Hoax : in Remedial Education : 7 : 3 : 9-10

Lewis, I. and Vulliamy, G. (1980) "Warnock or Warlock?" The Sorcery of Definitions : Educ. Rev.

Lynch, J. and Burns, B. (1984) Non-Attenders at INSET Functions : Journal of Education for Teaching : 10 : 2

Nash, R. (1975) Classrooms Observed : The Teachers' Perceptions and the Pupils' Performance : Routledge

Swann, W. (1984) "Integration Myth Dispelled" Article in T.E.S. : 15 : 6 : 84

Tomlinson, S. (1982) A Sociology of Special Education : Routledge and Kegan Paul

Welton, J. et al (1982) Meeting Special Educational Needs : Bedford Way Papers : London Institute

INDEX

Index